ABOUT MY EXPERIENCES IN LIBYA

A delightful book that will put us in contact with Libya

Leonor Massanet

2013

leonormassnaet@gmail.com

ISBN-13 978-1505721201
ISBN-10 1505721202

Edited: createspace.com (Amazón)

Translator: Debora Middleton
    debinmallorca@yahoo.com
Translated from original title: Relatos sobre mi experiencia en Libia

Acknowledgements

First of all, I wish to thank Osama Abubaker Al Nwir, without whom I would never have written this book, for his help in going to Libya, his dedicated guidance throughout the years and specifically for the way he welcomed me into the heart of his marvelous family which I now consider my own. And, of course, I wish to thank Osama for all his stories about his tribe, his life, as well as the enormous help he gave me inside Libya so that I could fulfill my goals.

And to all my Libyan family who welcomed me as one of them, making me feel completely at home.

Infinite thanks go to Purificación González de la Blanca, lawyer, writer, radio and TV political commentator, for her unconditional support, enthusiasm and assistance with the revisions to my manuscript. I realize that it was a great deal of work and she has given me her support and advice on this, my first literary effort.

To my family, especially my son, Marc, for reading successive versions of the manuscript and providing insight that has been so helpful to me. Also to my husband for being so patient with my questions about the computer, helping a lot to edit the book and giving me a lot of advices

Foreword:

Leonor, or the power of one

"My Experiences in Libya" by Leonor Massanet is an enchanting read that introduces us to Libya through the simple things in everyday life and to the culture and ways of a Mediterranean people who, like Libya, are relatively close, yet unknown, and who at one time, were practically living in paradise.

Leonor writes from the heart in a straightforward way, without embellishment, telling us about her experiences in this country that she loves so much: Libya, so close yet so far, that welcomed her with open arms to the point of its assimilating her (as well she becoming assimilated herself) into a Libyan family that she now considers "her" family.

Some of her anecdotes are delightful and recounted in a literary style reminiscent of Giovanni Guareschi, for its spontaneity and candour when describing certain situations whether embarrassing or amusing, and for the individuals in the story who, even when they are on the verge of explosively venting their fury, actually end up revealing their noble characters. Nobody is bad. Everyone is good. Some moments leave us with our hearts in our mouths, as when she tried to immortalize a wedding in a photograph and, as the flash goes off, it looked as if the world were falling apart. At other times, she launches herself, without parachute, into the unknown with a delightful desire to integrate which takes her into the bosom of the Walit family, who are friends with her own, and with whom she cannot communicate in any language. Nevertheless, they dress her as a typical Libyan woman which she not only allows them to do but also, with no idea as to how she should behave, goes with the flow and drives with them through the streets until they arrive at the studio of an Egyptian photographer who takes her portrait draped in jewellery amongst a colorful backdrop of divans, rugs, pitchers and tea services, looking perfectly at ease, even happy, as if she had been posing for the cameras all her life.

There are other amusing anecdotes like the day her friend, Osama, threw her out into the street so that she could finally get tired of looking at all the shops. All of this takes place against the backdrop of everyday life where the Libyans' concept of time put the author's nerves to the test virtually on a daily basis. Here we differ but, as a man in the desert once put it, "You have watches and we have time."

Throughout the entire book you literally breathe its humanity, its desire to inform, to break down taboos, sweep away all the prejudices, misunderstandings and even the lies about Muslim culture that have been disseminated over the centuries.

"My Experiences in Libya" is also a revealing book in which we discover how much we have in common with the Libyan people, to whom Leonor extends a hand of love.

It is a tender, simple and unified world that Leonor describes. One in which the Libyans did not want for material things because they had raised their country to the highest level of human development in all of Africa. One day this was destroyed by the plans of the colonial powers. For a long time the only reliable information that we had in Ojos para la Paz, as far as what was happening in Libya, came from this woman and her successful blog "leonorenlibia". Even today, she continues to inform us on what is happening there, in the face of the media silence that has been imposed as regards this country. These topics, however, have been deliberately omitted from the book because, as she believes and the Libyans themselves maintain, "we need to stop writing about what humiliates us because that is what will destroy us," and because we must not talk of the past but instead of "men and women who together are ready to build a new tomorrow".

We should do this. We must do this.

Purificación González de la Blanca
Ojos para la Paz
Cadiz, ,October 2013

Introduction

Throughout this book it is my intention is to bring the Libyan culture closer to the reader while enjoying, I hope, anecdotes of my experiences or those relayed to me during my stay in this country which I love so much: Libya

Despite the fact that Libya is on the Mediterranean coast only two hours away by plane from Madrid, most people I have spoken to are not even aware of its geographical location.

Its historical and cultural characteristics, together with the embargo and isolation to which it has been unjustly subjected, have brought about a very distinctive culture that even when speaking the same language, would require the help of a cultural spokesperson to understand it.

The Libyans preserve their ancestral customs while they go, or have gone, to university. They have information on the world at large thanks to satellite TV in all their homes, they speak languages, travel for their university studies or post graduate degrees... All of this produces a singular and passionate mix which is really worth getting to know.

A country with a unique, special and marvelous people.

About my experiences in Libya

My Arrival

Landing in Tripoli and being met by my friends was thrilling for me. As I would find out later, their courtesy, discretion and hospitality did not give me the feeling of being different. I always felt completely at home.

I arrived on my own at Tripoli airport and I went through all the usual airport procedures but at no time did I feel lost or disoriented as there was always someone ready to smile and help me out without my having to make any effort to make myself understood.

I was supposed to travel south where I was going to live with a very large family to begin my immersion and observation into the personality and relationship development of children as a result of their family environment, since my doctoral work for my career in psychology dealt with this subject. My thesis was that, since these were tribal families, the children were in constant contact with many family members. For this reason, I hoped to come across key indicators that would serve as a model to continue studying the development of a child's personality in different types of families up to and including western single-parent families.

I thought that I knew a lot about Libya, its culture, the way of life, the religion and, for this reason, I was not expecting any great surprises. I therefore proposed to do nothing more than go with the flow and observe. I felt comfortable and safe amongst them and whatever transpired would be welcome. I only needed to try to fit into their lives as best I could so that they would accept me as one of them.

Obviously, I could never imagine the great differences that I was already experiencing and those that I was not yet even aware of in spite of my joint degree in psychology and pharmacology.

At the airport my friend Osama and his older brother Mohamed were waiting for me with his two oldest sons. They welcomed me with great warmth, courtesy and, above all, very naturally.

I don't know if it is the calm of the desert which they carry in their genes, but one of the things that I have always appreciated about them is their ability to welcome you or begin a conversation as if they have known you before or had just seen you and at the same time were interested in you. I would say because of their culture and way of life, that they have exceptional social skills.

We got into the Toyota 4 x 4 in the airport parking lot. I felt happy, relaxed and ready to start this experience to which I had so looked forward.

The car became immersed in the streets of Tripoli until it finally stopped in front of a house. I could not tell you whether it was in the northern or southern part of the city after driving through such a labyrinth of streets. We were welcomed by a middle-aged man who looked very similar to those who had met me at the airport and it turned out he was another one of my friends' brothers. We

went into the house and they showed me into a room.

It was very spacious and full of light with the floor covered with wall-to-wall carpeting, or a large rug, with large cushions all around the walls. They gestured for me to sit on the floor, which I did.

Looked around and realized that the room did not have any pictures, tables or ornaments anywhere and yet I felt in a very welcoming place full of people.

People make a home, not things. This is possibly one of the most important basic principles that divides us from each other on these occasions and which touched my heart the most.

I sensed that nobody I had met before was in the room. Some young women with small children talked to me, asking questions, smiling and then they left and others arrived.

3

People kept coming and going. Everyone was very kind and always talking, asking me about my trip, my family, hundreds of questions that I was happy to answer when I understood them, while I also tried asking them their names, ages or things relating to their comments, even though I was unable to remember everything from so many people all at once.

For hours I stayed in that room not knowing where I was and what was going to happen next, as I had not seen Osama again since we had arrived at the house where I was never left alone. Then they came in with a serving dish of food, a salad, fruit, drink and various types of bread and some spoons.

They told me to eat and, since it was late and I was quite hungry, I did so and enjoyed it very much. The meal was very similar to our food although still different and tasty without my noting too much those spicy flavours that are so characteristic of Arab countries. It was light and very good.

The ingredients were exactly what we use since we are Mediterranean countries with similar cuisines; even the spices were very familiar. However, they are cooked in a different way. There was water and juices to drink. The water was rather interesting because it smelled of roses, which, however, did not alter its taste. Some time later I learned that they add drops of rosewater essence to give it such a special fragrance.

Afterwards, with all the naturalness in the world, they asked me if I would like to take a shower. I was a little nervous about what I should say as this was the first time I had ever taken a shower while a guest in someone's house. After a few moment's reflection, I decided that it would be better to take advantage of opportunities as they arose as I did not know when the next one would come along or when I would have another chance to take a shower.

Once clean and smelling like a rose, I returned to the room and continued chatting with a large number of people who kept coming and going. To tell the truth, I began to get confused as to who was who because there were so many people in such a short time. The parents, their daughters with their respective husbands, single men, single women, aunts, uncles, nieces, nephews, grandchildren... Later on I learned that I had been in the family home of the wife of a brother from the family with whom I was going to live. It was simply that they had asked to see me to get to know me since I was going to live with their family and it was only natural that I visit them. For them, everything was so obvious and normal that no explanation was needed, however, I only found this out some time after living in Libya.

Anything remotely important is discussed by members of the extended family, that is to say, the tribe. It was therefore logical that they knew I was coming and wanted to say hello to me.

Suddenly, in the afternoon they told me they were waiting for me outside to take me south. I left, happy to continue on my journey and to see my friends again whom I could "interrogate" to my heart's content. I had so many questions for them.

My first question was, "Where have we been"? Osama's calm and relaxed answer was that we had been in the family home of the wife of his older brother Abderahman.

I noted that they were not hiding anything, that they were talking about things and I felt that if they did not say anything more it was because there was nothing untoward.

I did not know how to ask, without being a nuisance or rude, why we had gone to that house, why he had not warned me and where had they been all that time…. I had so many questions I wanted to ask. I thought, however, that I would have all the time in the world to ask them and that, little by little, I would come to know the reasons for a behavior that appeared strange to me but which, instinctively, I felt was totally normal for them.

I could understand that his older brother and his family would come to the airport to meet me. I could also understand that the other older brother wanted to invite us to eat. But to spend all day in the family home of the wife of the brother, and my friends disappearing… There I felt that I had reached the limit of my understanding.

In reality, and I learned this little by little, the Libyans' lives revolve around their family and tribe and their relationships are steady and very close. For this reason, it was natural that my friend, Osama, his older brother and sons come to meet me at the airport. Similarly it was perfectly normal for the second son of the family to want to know who I was and therefore spend some time together.

As he, his wife and children were living in the family house of his wife at that time, they considered it natural that we should go there. Furthermore, his wife's family were pleased to see us.

For us, a visit to the family of the wife of a brother of mine, for example, would entail an invitation beforehand with enough time to take a gift, etc. However, the Libyans live immersed in this great tribal network so it was normal for all the closest members of the tribe to know that I was arriving and that, before going south, we would stop and meet them. It would even have been quite normal for us to have stayed one or two days. Afterwards, I also found out that other people had been expecting a visit from us too but that my hosts, Osama and Ibrahim, thought that I would not be used to so many visits and I could find that too much, especially on the first day of my arrival after having spent a whole day flying.

On reading about these personal experiences, one could think that so much curiosity and kindness over somebody new might be the result of having nothing better to do. I believe nothing could be further from the truth because these are very well educated people with many family ties. They speak English better than most. A great many have enjoyed further education and they talk with knowledge and respect about other cultures, countries and religions. For this reason, conversations are pleasant and wide-ranging from the daily gossip (they cook beans here too) to a subject that might be of topical interest.

They master the art of dialogue with great skill and this is something that endeared them to me and which I loved about them right from the start because I enjoy connecting with people, through both listening and talking. Perhaps this is the first thing that attracted me to the Libyans and which motivated me to want to keep on interacting and getting to know them better.

From satellite TV, they know perfectly well how the western consumer society works since they have access to both western and Arab channels, so they see everything - American and European programmes, just the same as us, Egyptian, Syrian, Iranian shows or programmes from other Arab countries. However, Libya was only knocking at the door, by this I mean still a fledgling consumer society, having lived in isolation for so many years.

A Libyan friend of mine, who had just finished her degree in biology, spoke very good English and had learned and perfected it from watching American TV shows.

They like Egyptian films but say that they are a little irritating because they are based on U.S. propaganda. The Syrian shows are the best because they reflect real life in that country including their characteristic sense of humour. Jordan makes the best Bedouin programmes. Algeria makes educational films such as, for example, a family who goes to live in the west and encounters many cultural differences... They also watch TV shows from Saudi Arabia, Lebanon, Kuwait and Bahrain.

I remember when I was a young girl, in the evenings my brothers and sisters and I would sit out on the terrace with our parents chatting and star gazing. We spent hours letting our ideas, dreams and thoughts flow uninterrupted, completely relaxed as my father taught us the names of stars or told us a story from his childhood or from the civil war. Now television, computers, all this new technology plus a consumer society have turned us all into robots. Socialising with people has been replaced by interacting with machines.

We began the journey south towards the home where I was to live throughout my stay in Libya. I asked a lot of questions. I did nothing except ask questions.

One of my first questions was how long would we take to get to the house where I would be lodging and the reply was "several hours". Then came my second question which was how many kilometers would we have to drive to get there, to which they replied about 800 Km. as if it were only 30 Km. With this new piece of information, I fell silent because to them it was never a question of inconveniencing anyone.

Libya is a vast country almost three times the size of Spain (1,775,000 Km2) and with only six million inhabitants. It is very spread out where distances are always great and the people are used to making long journeys. Also, among other things, everyone has a car and the petrol is virtually free. Obviously, no matter how good they were as hosts, they could not possibly imagine that I live in the Mediterranean on an island called Mallorca where, if you tried to go more than 80 Km in a straight line, you would end up in the sea.

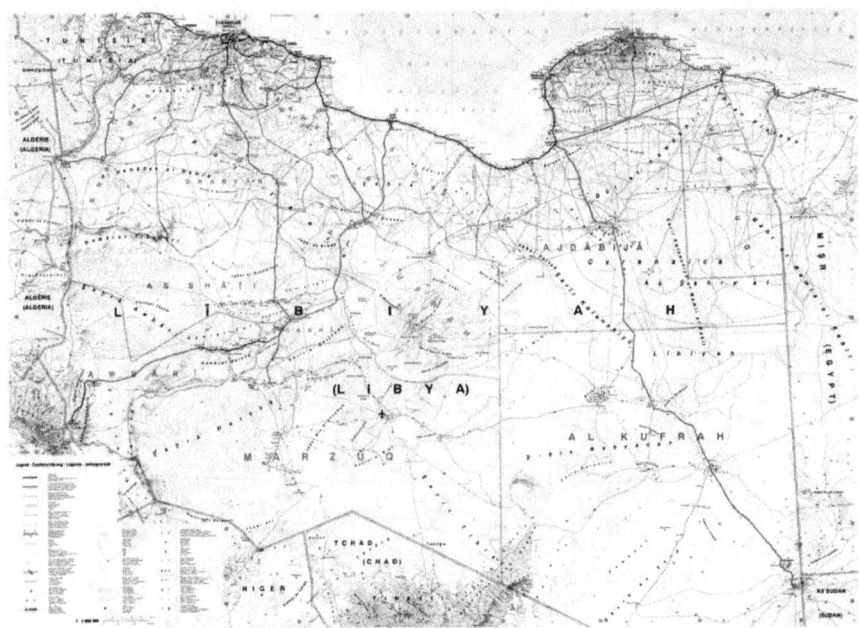

The journey took at least six hours but it did not feel long as I had a lot of questions and everything seemed new and wonderful to me.

I was going to stay with Osama's older sister, Minna, together with her husband and six children.

Osama

I believe the moment has come to explain how I came to travel to Libya and who Osama is, the person who helped make my dream come true and who was my guide and advisor every time I needed it and who is now my brother and whose family is my family.

When I made the decision to go to Libya, for several months I did everything to try and contact people or organizations in Libya in order to visit the country and begin my research and observations within a Libyan family, in keeping with the project that I had set myself to do for my doctorate. However, for some reason which I still do not understand, I was unable to make contact with anyone until I called my friend, Osama, and explained what I was looking for. In a few days he returned my call to tell me that he had found the ideal family for my research/observations, that is to say, my field of work. What he did not tell me at first was that it involved his sister, Ismahan.

Osama is a genuine man of the desert. Born in the desert, he has spent his entire life there, even though, at the same time, he travelled and studied for several years at university. He did not finish his studies and, according to his family, this was due to his friendships but later I learned that the reasons were much more complex. He did do several modules and went to Ireland to study English for a year, obviously paid for by the government.

He is a man of great analytical capabilities and highly creative. He knows the Sahara like the back of his hand and would never become lost in it. He is like a walking GPS. It is as if he were a part of the Sahara, capable of getting everything necessary from these arid regions.

We traveled the entire Libyan Sahara from north to south, east to west with our mutual friend, Mohamed, and we never found ourselves in a situation that gave me cause for concern while I'm sure, had I been alone, I would have died several times a day.

I knew him and we became good friends to the point that he told me many things about his family, girlfriends, personal conflicts etc. And, possibly, he was responsible for igniting in me the desire to go to Libya and research more and more.

As a good Libyan born in the heart of the Sahara, he lived for his group and this is the characteristic that compelled him to be a good host to any guests which was exactly what I was. I was able to see first hand to what extent and how far they are prepared take this cultural behavior.

He was 41 years old and this made him a witness to the changes that Libya had experienced, especially the Libyan Sahara, from the time when there was constant tribal warfare and they lived in poverty, to the present day phase of peace, security and well-being.

I asked him to help me integrate into his culture and his home. I told him that I would do everything he asked of me with pleasure and he accepted this responsibility with good grace. I can say that he was my teacher and counsellor whom I called thousands of times for advice, who would explain a situation, or facts, or what he believed I should do in a particular situation. He always knew how to advise me up to the point that you could say he could become a little bit of a "pain", because it is always difficult to immerse yourself in such a different culture without making hundreds of mistakes.

His sister's husband, Ali, had studied his master degree in

England and logically went with the whole family on a grant from the Libyan government. When he left for England he had only one child, but came back with six children all speaking perfect English, thanks to the fact they all received a benefit from the government, which was their due, as Libyans. A great privilege which surprised me a lot.

It was the ideal family for me as they lived in Wadi Ash Shati, in the middle of the Sahara, to the northwest of Sabha, deep inside Libya.

At the same time, they had only returned from England a few months earlier and therefore thought that I would feel more comfortable with them and we would get used to each other more easily.

Now I remember when I was waiting to travel to Libya, I asked Osama on the telephone to tell me where exactly I was going to live. I bought a map of Libya and tried for several days to find Wadi Ash Shati but with no luck. My Spanish family kept asking me for specific information as to where I would live, what I would be doing, and many other things. I only knew the approximate location and that was all I could tell them. I remember trying to imagine where I was going to live and what the family would be like and what my life would be like with that family but I did not have enough information, not by a long shot, to imagine what my future would hold.

During the trip towards Wadi Ash Shati, Osama explained details about his family, their names, ages and certain characteristics of each one of them. On realizing how many of them there were, I was not able to remember their names so I picked up pen and paper and wrote them all down. In Osama's family there were 15 siblings, three of whom I already knew, and I would live in the home of a fourth sister.

He surprised me when telling me the name of each brother, sister, niece or nephew as he would always explain the meaning of their name. I had never wondered about the meaning of my own name, if it did mean anything, and it struck me as very special that people, on giving a name to their child, did it to remember a person, idea, scenery, feeling or even something cosmic such as, for example, "Torayah" which means a constellation of stars.

Already from that moment in the Toyota on the way to the Libyan Sahara I began to understand a language, culture and history that was full of symbolism, all within a huge, tight-knit social network.

The 800 km between Tripoli and Wadi Ash Shati passed almost without my realizing it as I kept on writing since I was incapable of remembering so many names, especially when they were so different from ours. Furthermore, most of them were unknown to me and I was hearing them for the very first time.

I remember that there was a moment in which I thought that simply learning the names, ages, relationship and placing everyone was like a new language. Osama spent a lot of time talking to me about everybody that I was going to meet but there came a moment when my brain became completely saturated and I simply wrote down everything he told me about each person.

I tried to focus as much as I could on Minna, Ali and their six children with whom I was going to live in Wadi Ash Shati.

Finally, around three o'clock in the morning, we arrived at our destination. On entering the house, they took me straight to a large carpeted room with cushions all around, a television and a table with a chair. Two adorable little girls were waiting for us there with their parents, Ali and Minna.

One of the little girls gave me a picture she had drawn and we sat down to talk. I still have that drawing because it was very important to me when that little 8 year old, so pretty and sweet, gave me the drawing that she had been making for me as a sign of welcome to her home, even though she had yet to meet me. We all sat down in the living room and began to talk quietly about the trip, how I was, about the family that we had visited and generally about everything that had happened on my first day in Libya. They chatted as if it had been 12 o'clock in the afternoon and this was also a surprise that intrigued me for a long time until I understood the reason.

Another surprise was to find out that the same room where they had received me was going to be my bedroom and private space. I did not know that and would never have guessed since up until that day I had always slept in a bed.

In Libya these rooms are used for daily life and at night they place small mattresses on the carpet and blankets as necessary and you sleep beautifully. Our translation from a western standpoint would be a "flexible" room.

Later I grew to understand the usefulness of these flexible rooms.

The couple have their own bedroom and nowadays they all have a large bed, wardrobe, dressing table etc.

There are several large rooms with a mountain of mattresses for the rest of the family and guests because every day family members visit and these are not just one guest but can be up to 10 people, more or less, so that when night falls, they just spread out the mattresses in the rooms and everyone goes to sleep. Usually the women sleep together with the children and the men sleep in separate rooms.

They told me that I had the use of a room for myself with a table in western style including a TV, so that I was like a queen and when they left me to rest, I think I fell asleep almost immediately, comfortable and happy.

One Surprise after Another

My next surprise came the very next day.

On waking up, I naturally immediately went to the toilet. However, I was surprised that these people who were so hospitable were so "forgetful" and had not placed toilet paper or towels in the bathroom. In my home it would have been unthinkable to forget such things but I was not there to judge and I had an easy solution as I had hygienic paper wipes and a towel in my suitcase. I got dressed again in order to get them and everything was resolved.

I remember that I thought that quite likely, with so many children, there might have been a misunderstanding.

I needed a refreshing shower after the trip and the heat in the middle of August in the Sahara so I got in the shower and turned on the tap. Ahhhh! The water was boiling! I let it run for a moment to see if it was the pipe that was hot but it never got any cooler. Afterwards they told me to try and shower either early in the morning or at night because during the day the water in the tanks was so hot that it was impossible to wash or shower with it.

The water tanks are on top of the houses in temperatures of more than 50 C degrees in the summer.

I was grateful for this information and never told them that I had figured that out for myself that same morning when I could not take a shower.

During the three days that I spent in that house, I never asked for a towel or toilet paper and nobody ever mentioned them. I felt that these issues were a little intimate and did not want to bother them or make them feel that, despite their hospitality, they had forgotten something. I directed most of my questions to the children because they were always around me and were very open and attentive. I felt comfortable with them, without formalities and at the same time they tried to help me telling me the problems I could have if I rested under the large shady tree in the garden, a little like a Jacaranda but with red flowers, because a scorpion could fall on me! A scorpion! Well, this was a huge surprise for me, however, I must say that it was years before I saw one up close.

Scorpions can be found only in rubbish and damp farm areas and never in the desert with its dry sand. Most of the farmers have been stung by a scorpion and they know what they must do when this happens. Everything depends on the very painful sting. The Libyans are not afraid of scorpions. They explained that the sting is more or less dangerous depending on the size of the scorpion and how long it has been since it expelled any poison. The smaller the scorpion, the more virulent it is.

On several occasions, I heard about how people I knew had been stung by a scorpion as if they were talking about a bee sting.

By this, I mean, they did not give it that much importance.

The first scorpion that I saw was brought to me in a glass jar and left on the ground (photo above) for me to enjoy.

They told me that when a scorpion stings them, they quickly make themselves bleed to remove the poison. The more you bleed, the better. They actually make a small cut close to the area so as to bleed as much as possible. Afterwards, you feel a strong pain that extends through the body as the poison spreads but they also say that this allows them to know how far it is progressing, so they know more or less how much time they have to get to the hospital for the antidote.

Some of the best information I would get from the children because they also came from England and most of them had been born over there, so they had been through the same thing as me, albeit slightly differently and from a child's perspective. They understood that I could be surprised by things and might find the way of life quite different. There was never any need for me to ask them to come and explain many of the things that we were experiencing.

Much later while already living in the family home of all the siblings, I became good friends with the three youngest sisters who were studying at university. They explained how you clean yourself in the toilet which cleared up the reason why there was no toilet paper. I then understood why I had seen the taps and small hand held sprays in the toilets. I felt so stupid for not having picked up on something so natural and, at the same time, I liked the solution.

Every time you go to the toilet there are small hoses and a tap, right next to you, for cleaning yourself. It is much better than how we do it with toilet paper. I liked it so much that when I returned to my house in Mallorca, I installed this system.

It was more difficult for me to understand the issue of the towel. The Sahara is such a dry environment that there is no need for a towel in the summer. Although you may not believe it, you simply shower and start to dress because you are already dry. The first few times it seemed impossible or as if I were doing something wrong. I have to admit, however, that it works perfectly and is even pleasant because it is so hot that as the water evaporates, it leaves you refreshed. There is a moment when the body is dripping as you finish the shower and then the next step is just to step out of the tub and start dressing. It seems crazy, especially with wet skin, but actually you are fine and dry by the time you leave the bathroom.

The differences had not ended with these small things and would continue.

My first day in the house was very pleasant with six children who were interested in learning, well behaved and who spoke perfect English. The oldest boy was 12 years old and the youngest girl was 2 or 3 years old.

I loved to watch how close-knit they all were; how the older ones always looked after the smaller ones and how the little ones listened and asked for help from them, on a hierarchical scale of responsibilities. Each one expected help from the older one who is guide to the younger one.

Later, I learned that that same pecking order is carried on all through life even though it becomes simply a code of behavior.

I also learned that it is not always as idyllic as I first thought because people all over the world have weaknesses and "mortal sins" are not exclusive just to Christians.

I noticed, however, a great respect for one another. This is a statement that requires much greater explanation because at the end of the day people are all the same in any culture. Jealousy and envy or any type of feelings positive or negative accompany human beings wherever their place of birth, but what is true is that by being such large communities and living together with so many people, they are used to respecting the space of each one without stepping on one another and they have devised many ways of settling these problems.

The same thing happens with food because all the families eat from the same tray which is placed in the centre of them. It might appear complicated because there may be one who takes a larger share than another or someone who could annoy you... I can think of many things I could say without having ever experienced them. However, there I realized that there was an order and respect and each one ate from the space in front of him and did not touch the food of the others. It is something that they do every day and I never felt uncomfortable with it nor heard any discussion about it.

I like the fact they know how to work and live together: they know how to share.

There was also another small issue: sitting on the ground to eat without my foot touching the cloth. Even though it may seem strange from our culture of table and individual plate, in reality there are clears rules of good behavior and hygiene with regard to sitting down as well as eating.

They love juices and they always accompany meals with apple juice, tropical fruit, orange and banana or pineapple juices. Some even contain pieces of fruit and taste very natural. I love more than anything to drink water and always had to ask for it because they would always place a juice in front of you and insist that you drank it. I think that they like them so much that it was hard for them to understand that I did not particularly like them. Sometimes I drank them so as not to disappoint them and make them think they were not good hosts.

I have never been able to fathom out this devotion to juice or French bread or a few other things. Although I believe they are products that came to Libya after the U.S.A. lifted the embargo and thanks to that many more western products began to arrive in Libya. This is somewhat similar to what happened to us in Spain when French cheese, Swiss chocolate and many other food products arrived that seemed to us to be the ideal.

Libyan Green Tea

What I like best is its green tea. It is exquisite with its froth, served in a small glass. Libyan tea is not an infusion like we make but they boil it for at least half an hour and often add other very aromatic desert plants which give it a very special flavour. Sugar is added directly into the teapot before serving so there is no choice but to drink it sweet but it is delicious.

Once it has been boiled it is poured from one vessel to another to make the froth that will fill half the glass before adding the tea.

Tea made this way is highly concentrated and for that reason it is understandably drunk in smaller quantities than our cups. I have never seen them add any kind of mint to it.

As I was used to Moroccan mint tea or Egyptian tea with its

peppermint, I was surprised that in Libya they did not follow the same custom. Once again my mind was following western ethnocentrism and making generalizations.

The herbs that they add are always during boiling.

Due to our cultural tendency for oversimplification and our belief in other generalizations and biases introduced to us by the media, we treat all Arab countries as one, as if they were all alike, ate the same food, believed, dressed and behaved in the same way. It would be the same as if, for example, the Libyans believed that the Spanish have the same customs as the Norwegians, British or Estonians. I asked them why they did not use peppermint in their tea which would be tantamount to asking an Englishman why he did not make gazpacho instead of drinking tomato juice.

Osama, with all the patience and naturalness in the world told me that peppermint in Libya is given to teenagers in schools because it lowered the libido. Honestly, I did not know what to say because I had always thought that peppermint had the opposite effect but it would not be proper to question his beliefs. However, in retrospect, I think his answer was only an imaginative tall story just to say something as I have never heard this explanation in Libya about peppermint.

Sometimes I think I used to ask my friends, especially Osama, so many questions that at times he would sometimes invent an answer. At least I could always turn to his sisters who were delighted to explain everything I asked them.

Meals

Libyans eat with their hands, helped along by bread. I have to confess that I found it a little difficult to take on board the fact that people in the civilized world with university careers could eat with their hands because, in my house, it was forbidden to use your hands for eating as it was considered bad manners. My mother was always very strict on table manners, and not being allowed to use your hands was one of the basic rules. However, in Libya in the main room there is a sink for washing before praying and also before and after eating. For this and other reasons I have to say that they are extremely clean people.

Before seating themselves around the food, they wash their hands, then they eat with the bread and their hands but according to their own standards, which is normal, and their own table manners.

The only cutlery that they use, when they use it, and which they gave to me, was a spoon for everything. I never saw a knife or fork at a Libyan meal except once when I ate in a high ranking house at a engagement meal.

Once the meal has been finished, they wash their hands and mouth with care. These are rituals which I saw everybody I have met do, including when going to restaurants. When finished they get up to wash.

The way of eating is to place a tablecloth on the rug and then they place the food on the cloth. The diners then sit around the tablecloth.

I had to learn how to sit down and at one point I had to ask my friends to help me and asked them to please tell me whenever I made a mistake. It is not easy to sit down around the cloth, take the food with your hands and spoon and not touch the cloth with your foot.

Everything is actually easy when you try and use your five senses but eating, chatting and passing the time, I do not know how but I always managed that my toes ended up touching the tablecloth. I finally learned not to do that and to feel comfortable like they did around the tablecloth.

The means were very similar during most of the work week. They were healthy and at the same time tasty.

There were always small plates of cucumbers, tomato and finely chopped peppers seasoned with salt and lemon. Plates of melon and watermelon or other seasonal fruit and a big plate of couscous or rice or pasta with meat which would normally be chicken or lamb.

Eggs are eaten in the morning in a sort of scrambled egg with tomato and peppers. The peppers that I have seen in Southern Libya are certainly hot.

Sometimes instead of a central dish of couscous, they make a Libyan soup, lentils or spaghetti.

Then there are meals for special occasions or weddings like Fta, Basin, Batan and many more which are more tasty and similar to our dishes.

The taste of the salads is surprising and, with almost no dressing, have a wonderful flavor and the water which smells of roses but is tasteless... the food is not overly seasoned so that I never was surprised by any strange flavor but, on the contrary, it always seemed familiar to me as if I had been eating it all my life.

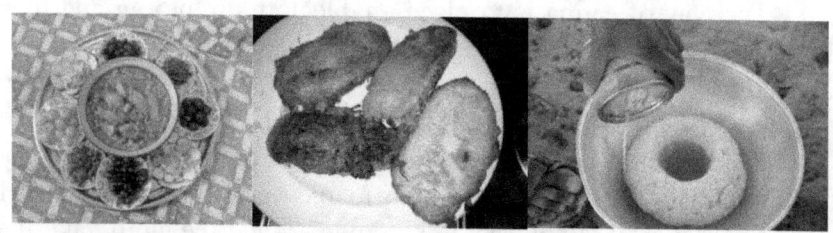

The Family and its Schedule

The life of a family with six children was quite easy and I only had to let myself go with the flow as the children had just come back from England and I did not surprise them at all and furthermore they spoke perfect English just like their parents. There were also six children in my family as well.

However, three days after my arrival I was faced with a dilemma because the grandparents of the children wanted me to go and live with them, by this I mean in the house of the parents of my friends, because that way we could see more of each other and I would also have the opportunity to see many more children. They told me that it was my decision but I had no idea as at that point I had only been in Libya for three days and I only knew the home where I was staying.

I can imagine what happened, all those over at the family homestead listening to what the family members in Tripoli who had met me were telling them, about my stay with the family where I was living, about Osama... For sure the parents would have to ask me to go and live there and that way we could all see each other more often.

I went to my friends, Osama and Ibrahim and told them to do what they thought was best, that I would was using them as my guides and would accept whatever decision was best for me and the family. They then explained that the family was asking me to go there because all the single sisters and those married with children also wanted to meet me and share time with me so they advised me to go over there because there I would see everyone, including the family with whom I was currently living. It was the home of the grandparents with 15 children where the two eldest with their children I had met in Tripoli lived and they were around 40 years old.

In the family home there were 8 single children still living there while the rest were married with children and visited often, staying several days.

Before leaving the first house I needed to know a few things: the schedule.

My friends telephoned to say that the following day they would come to get me and take me to the family home and that I should have my bags packed. Obviously, my first question was "what time?". The reply was clear, "Around ten"... and since, at that time, I still kept to my western timetables, I unwaveringly accepted this as fact. Early the next morning I packed all my clothes into my suitcase, showered and went out to chat to the children. They asked me to go outside into the garden to play with them with bats and balls because we had not entertained ourselves much the day before, but I told them that I could not because I had just showered and they would be coming to pick me up. They told me that they did not care and that we should go out and play but I, with my western mentality, put it down to childishness that they wanted to play with me.

The reality was quite different because I ended up waiting without wanting to become sweaty and with the suitcase packed until three or four o'clock in the afternoon. Around this time Osama and Ibrahim, happy and carefree, with no feelings of guilt and with no apology for the difference between the agreed 10 o'clock in the morning (according to my point of view) and the time they actually arrived of 4 o'clock in the afternoon. When they came into the house, they greeted us and told me to get my luggage. My western instinct wanted me to ask what had happened between 10 o'clock and 4 0'clock, however, my intuition advised me to simply go with the flow and I would find out and learn about this way of life.

Yes, it is one of the hardest differences to get used to except if you forget the western system and totally embrace this one because there, they never wait for anybody. What I should have done is simply carry on with my normal day until they got there and if they had to wait for me for a couple of minutes it would have been perfectly normal because they had to talk a little with the family and tell them the latest news. They probably simply got up in the morning, perhaps had to go and buy bread, then the father asked them to fix something with the car, on finishing a guest arrived who needed to be looked after, then it was lunchtime and with those high temperatures it was not advisable to travel the 80 km that they would have to drive to pick me up, so they ate and had a little siesta until it cooled down. If I had known the customs of the south a little better, it would have been much easier because I would have carried on as usual without worrying about anything until they arrived at the house.

I have to admit that it is one of the things I had the most trouble adapting to because, without even wanting to, I am set in my ways learned over the years and keep doing things in a fixed timeframe. I do not even realize it and when they say "let's go shopping" I make the mistake of being ready in 5 minutes. Then, when half an hour has gone by and nobody is making a move to go, I understand that they are waiting for somebody who is busy with the baby or who is getting ready. However, those who are waiting just get on with what they are doing without worrying about it at all and I am the only one who has stopped what she is doing and put herself in waiting mode. However, once you manage to get used to this, it seems perfectly normal.

On arriving at the family home there was another even more difficult period of adaptation. In my first home I had managed to name and place everyone. At first I had a piece of paper in my hand and later I began to remember names with faces.

The problem was that now in the family home there were even more people and new families and children would arrive whom I had to meet and talk to. I am sure that I made many mistakes when talking with one or another because sometimes I did not know if I had already talked to them about a certain subject or whether it was with another.

I continued to learn the rules of cohabitation that were normal for them, such as removing your shoes before entering a house because Libyans go barefoot inside their homes. When they go into the toilet for reasons of hygiene, they always put on rubber flip flops.

These are very sensible rules that I respect a great deal, however, my mind was not always up to it and many times I came out of the bathroom wearing the flip flops and half an hour later realized that I had not taken them off or I would go into a home and with all the greetings would forget to remove my shoes. It happened many times until finally I acquired the habit and it became second nature to me. There was a moment when I realized that I was forgetting too many times and it could be construed as a lack of respect for their customs, however, nobody ever made a negative comment about it, except for some child who would remind me that I was wearing the flip flops from the bathroom or I was wearing my shoes in the house.

Since my lifelong customs seem completely natural to me and I would perhaps not recognize the need to explain why we do certain everyday things, I can equally understand that something that the Libyans do, and have done all their lives, is something that would not occur to them that I might not know, because the reality is that the same surprise that different ways give us, would be the same for them with regard to our ways.

One day Mannar told me that she and her sisters liked to watch how I handled the cutlery with such grace and dexterity. In truth, I have never considered that I could be graceful or skillful when using a knife and fork because I have done it all my life and it was something which my parents insisted on as good table manners.

I remember a western woman was highly offended because, in a recently opened hotel in Libya, she found no toilet paper in the bathroom. Her words were very cutting with regard to the service in Libya and it never occurred to her that she could wash herself with the shower spray next to the toilet. She went to reception, protested loudly and the Libyans gave their apologies. Within 10 minutes all the bathrooms had toilet paper. However, that lady continued telling everyone who would listen about the poor standard of service in the hotel, since on arrival they had found no toilet paper.

If this lady had lodged at an international hotel chain in any country in the world she would surely have found international services mingled with the local culture of that country. It must be said, however, that the Libyan hotel from that moment onwards had toilet paper for the westerners as well as the shower spray which is used for this purpose. That lady did not know how to notice many details, only the Libyan ones which made that hotel a special place, and she only knew how to make a comparison by finding what were, for her, faults.

The layout of Libyan houses and life within them

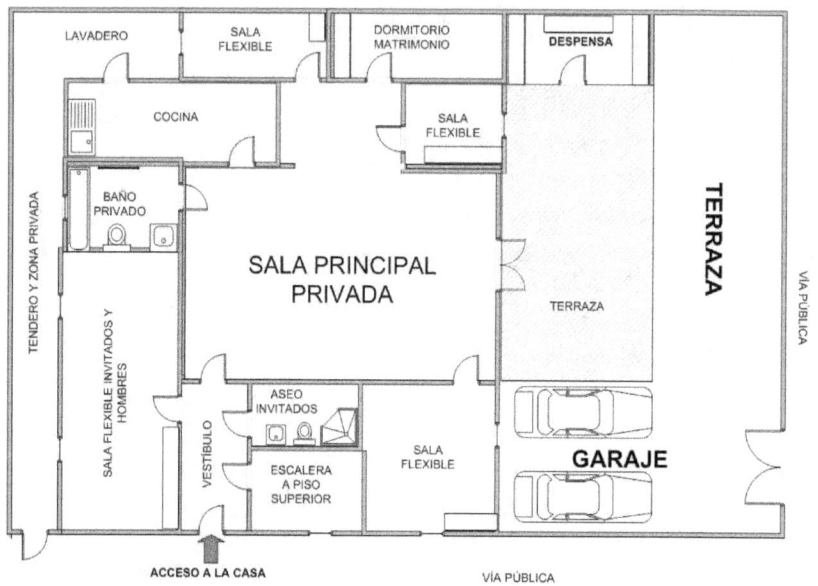

This plan relates to the family home where I lived for the majority of my stay in Libya. It is a limited plan and for the purpose of giving an idea of the layout of the rooms. The measurements are not actual ones.

On looking at the layout, you can see how private the lives are of the Libyans because most of the guests and men are only able to use the rooms designated for them such as the hallway, toilet and flexible room for guests. The immediate family, that is the brothers, sisters and children can go anywhere.

Trusted women and wives of brothers can also go anywhere in the house.

It may seem a large house; however, it belongs to a humble family. In Libya most of the houses are larger.

This organization which can be observed from afar as "harem style" because that is what the western media and literature have told us, has a much simpler explanation because it is a house in which many children and various married couples live and people can be in their pajamas or praying or feeding their babies or simply relaxing and chatting. It is impossible to give so many people their privacy.

There are daily visitors and many are people who are not such close friends so it is imperative to guard the intimacy of the family. When you live there on a daily basis you understand this perfectly and appreciate that the visitors stay in the room set aside for guests. This is yet another part of the social organization of people who live closely together and have been obliged to find ways of coexistence that work with their needs.

The husbands of invited families, that is to say the husbands of the married sisters, sleep separately from the women in the guest room. I understand that this can also be misconstrued. Yet again, the explanation speaks for itself because the Libyan homes are always large but not big enough to house privately all the couples that are in the house and this is why they designate rooms of flexible use so that they can house more people.

Everything is carpeted and every day they vacuum the house and clean the bathrooms and kitchen.

My best observation post was the central living room where there were always several women seated on the floor while their babies slept in their arms, or breast fed, or began to make their first tentative steps away from their mothers, or quickly went from mother to aunt and then back to mother again, or played with their little cousins around their mothers. All this while always respecting the pecking order placed on them by their ages. There I watched how babies would develop their independence in a natural way on their own initiative and with no pressure learning how to crawl and then to walk. It happened with an overwhelming naturalness because everyone was sitting on the floor and the child only had to climb off his mother's knees.

I hardly ever heard nervous mothers scolding their little children because it is hard to find a reason to do so. To begin with, there is no furniture or ornaments to touch or break and that is one of the most important reasons in our homes: "Don't touch that you might break it", "Don't climb on that chair, you might fall off", "careful because you are going to hurt yourself on the corner of the table"... None of these warnings would be necessary in a Libyan home.

The main living room had cushions all around and in the corner was a western style sofa, as decoration, which was a novelty and for this reason one of the children had bought it or given it to them. It was used as a resting place for the recently washed laundry, for folding and ironing, or to leave bags or telephones. It got used as more of a table. It was also useful because it had a plug just above the seat back and so was always full of everyone's telephone chargers.

Another novelty in many of the homes was a plastic porch chair which to them was something new and original. At first, because of my western way of thinking, I looked on it as something left inside the house by mistake but that could belong to the patio furniture. However, the chair never went outside and had the same kind of role as the sofa.

Actually, if we are sitting on the floor, positions change and it is handy to leave the telephone of the chair or sofa so that nobody will step on it.

With my western culture I found it hard to understand how they can study medicine or biology or some other university course seated on the ground. I would often watch them because I needed to carry on writing and making notes when I studied and sitting on the floor makes it hard to write. Obviously, I am referring to myself and never to the Libyans. At the end of the day they sit down and get up hundreds of times and I think this is the reason why they have such firm "derrieres". At times they squat with the soles of the feet completely flat on the ground and can stay like that for as long as they like.

I believe that getting up and sitting down on the ground so many times a day plus the stretching during prayer is great exercise that keeps them healthy, strong and agile. In reality, many of the religious rites (including the old ones from the Catholic Church) comprise a dose of yoga for this purpose.

They even do the ironing on the floor. They place a special ironing mat and the piece of clothing goes on top of that. Then they iron either kneeling or sitting on the floor.

I visited the house of some recently married friends of Osama who had a modern kitchen with all the cabinets around the room so as to be able to work in the western way. However, the new wife used the floor to decant pots or for some other food preparation. To my eyes it seemed strange and uncomfortable but obviously it was only me who held this point of view.

A few days after arriving at the family home I thought I would like to start reading the Koran in order to determine the relationship between certain customs of the country and the Koran like, for example, the fact that the women cover their faces which according to western thinking is a Muslim law. In fact, I found out that it is simply a custom in hot desert countries and came about to protect the skin of men as well as women and to protect them from the wind.

However, in the south you see as many men with their heads

covered as women including their faces. Even I cover myself when in the desert and many times during the day I covered my face too as the air is so dry and the sun so intense that your face becomes as dry as parchment. Libyan women take great care of their skin and wish to remain white so it is very important that not one ray of sunshine touches their face. They use whitening makeup instead of coloured foundations like we use. They were very surprised at my makeup and asked me why I used color.

The young girls who wanted to be different and watched western films would ask me for high factor sunscreen so they could go out in the sun without their skin tanning and without having to cover themselves. Other women avoid going outside at all costs while others cover their faces if they do.

Once I saw a friend with her face covered and since it was the first time I had seen anyone in Libya completely covered, I asked her why she did it. She told me that she did it because her husband made her. At that moment and with my western brainwashing, I believed her and felt that it was terrible. However, some time later I had the opportunity to spend several days with her husband in the same house with other family members and I realized that he was a calm, good natured, easy going man who was simple and down to earth. This surprised me a lot as I had formed a very different opinion of him. I asked him if it was true that he made his wife wear the veil. My friends laughed and asked me who had told me such nonsense. I told them that she had said so. The explanation that they gave me was that she had probably told me a little fib because she did not want to admit that it was out of vanity and to keep her face perfectly white because she is a little conceited.

It was a simple little white lie which in Libya only made my friends smile because of the vanity of this woman. In the west, however, it would serve as irrefutable proof of Arab male chauvinism.

I know a mother who never takes her child for a walk in the sun so that her son, in spite of living right in the Sahara, does not see the sun, even his pediatrician recommended that he take vitamin D and vitamin A like children who live in northern climates with little sunlight. No matter how many times I told her that her child would feel better if he only spent 5 minutes a day in the sun, I could not convince her because she did not want to go in the son and wanted her son to be as white as possible.

This is a sincere and private explanation that my friend disclosed to me but would never tell a stranger. Possibly she would say things like "my husband won't let me".

My First Purchase: A Koran

One of my first wishes was to buy a Koran because I realized  how important this book was to the Libyans. I wanted to know up to what point their behavior was based on Koranic directives, what things were imposed and what things were misinterpreted and many more questions that living with them seemed important for me to know and understand.

I went to Osama and asked if he could take me to a book store to buy a Koran to which he replied that of course he could whenever I wanted. I am sure that you have asked yourselves why I did not go out alone to look for a book store in the city and buy it myself. The answer to this requires a very long explanation which I hope to give but for now I prefer to tell you about my first purchase, if you can call it that.

We went with the car through a labyrinth of streets and houses which I could not identify, nor tell apart, streets without names or any particularly distinguishing features from each other, or at least it did not seem like it at first.

We drove around chaotically for several minutes without rules, stoplights, or traffic signals but always exercising mutual respect. At times it would seem that we were in the middle of a traffic jam which was impossible to get out of and then, little by little, each car made its way and slowly that great tangle of cars unraveled. We came to a place, he stopped the car, opened the door and got out saying, "Just a minute, I'll be back in a moment". After a few minutes he returned with the Koran in the above picture. A Koran written in Arabic and English so that on each page the text is in the two languages. He approached the car window where I was sitting waiting and asked me, "Is this what you want?"

I imagine that you can understand the number of questions and feelings that passed through my mind. To begin with, I did not know and could not see that we were in front of a book store. I was very curious to see a Libyan book store. My education and way of thinking stopped my from having an opinion on what he bought as I cannot compare it with others, since this was the first Koran I had ever seen in my life, without knowing what it was worth and compare. On the other hand, it seemed so strange that I stayed in the car.

I kept all these thoughts to myself because I wanted, above all, to live immersed in that family and that they accepted me into their lives without judging them. So I kept to myself the surging flood of feelings and ideas and simply asked, "What do you think? Why did you choose this particular one? How much is it?" He then explained it cost 6 dinars (1 euro = 1.7 LYD), that it was written in two languages, that it was the latest in this edition and the book store owner had told him it was the best. With this explanation and seeing that he made no move to invite me to get out of the car and choose for myself, I gave him the six LYD and ended up with my Koran which, when all is said and done, was what I wanted.

On returning home it took a while before I could go straight to my medical student friend to talk to her. I confide a lot in her and trust her completely and I told her everything that had happened. She listened to me with a smile of satisfaction then she asked if I liked the book I had bought and that she would like to see it too. Seeing that she did not understand my confusion, I admitted that I would have liked to have got out of the car, gone into the bookstore and chosen it myself etc. She was surprised and explained that I did not speak Arabic and that her brother had treated me like one of the family. In Libya men feel the need to show that the women in their families live like queens and this means that they "command" and the men obey and that if he had gone to buy me the Koran it was to make me feel good and help with things. She further explained that if I wanted to get out of the car, I should have told him. For sure, he would have been delighted to show me around the bookstore. Later

she told him herself so that he would take me to a bookstore and I could see what I would like.

I do not know if it is possible from outside to capture my point but my intention is to show how certain behaviors which in our eyes would be judged negatively due to all the information we have been

given about Arabs in general, are simply misinterpretations of very different cultures.

The first surprise for me was that the bookstore had no sign outside to say what it was. Although I must say that I did not know Arabic and if the word "BOOK STORE" had been written somewhere, I would not have recognized it anyway. During those first few days I had the impression that no shops indicated on the outside what they were selling, however, as time went by I began to change my opinion, or to understand better what I was seeing, or the shops were opening more, or a little bit of all of this. It is that Libya has changed a lot day by day, month by month, over the past few years.

A further problem was the language and the streets with no name or number on the houses. Osama told me that I was mistaken and that all the streets had a name but I never saw one. Perhaps it was known to all the inhabitants of the area but for me it was impossible to navigate in that city without a map. Many times I asked if I could get a map, and I even tried to get one on Google, but it was impossible because a home had grown larger as children married or siblings and family members had left to live nearby and leaving pathways between the houses which then gradually became wide streets. As the years went by, some of these homes changed owner and in this way a city large like Sabha, the capital of Fezzan, would be born.

Even though it seemed impossible to me, I decided that I would make my own map of the city once I had managed to orientate myself a little.

If I got lost, which was quite likely, I could not ask anybody for the house where I lived because such an address did not exist.

My friends told me to stop worrying and that each time I wanted to go out, I should tell the girls and they would take me where I wanted to go. Easy at first glance? However, again I must explain that in reality it was much more difficult than it would seem. In the first place we have to remember their attitude to timetables, which involved that just agreeing to go out could entail hours or even days depending on so many things. Then came the second part and that was how many people wanted to come with me. Unimaginable!

Children, pregnant women and anybody who wanted to would decide to join in. It was impossible follow any semblance of what I wanted to do when I had first asked about the possibility of going out for a walk because you had to stop at the pharmacy and buy something for a baby, or buy some shoes for another child or a thousand other things, since they were there.

I also remember that one of the women who made up the committee had to go to a wedding and needed to buy some appropriate clothes. She took advantage of our outing to go to several shops and perhaps buy the material and all the outfit. Actually, all of this was really interesting because through all these people I was understanding and learning about this very singular culture.

Even so I managed to go into a shop, note I say "shop" and not "shops" where they sold long dresses, pretty and comfortable which they wore in the house. I drew closer to have a look but obviously I had never seen them before and I did not know the different kinds, styles, types of material, prices etc to be able to go in, buy and leave. However, when I looked at one of the dresses they immediately asked me "Is this the one you want?" to which I responded that I did not know, that I was only looking and only wanted to know the price. They were a little nonplussed and talked amongst themselves because they did not understand my behavior.

Later I was told that it had seemed strange to them my way of going into the shops, looking around, asking, trying things on and then not buying because when they go in, they go in to buy and they already know more or less what they need or want and they were not as consumer oriented as we are.

They told me that my behavior had embarrassed them.

I have to explain, however, that they were changing their behaviour. I don't know when or how but we would go shopping and visit more and more shops without buying anything.

For years I was never able to go out shopping alone in Sabha. Having said this, it was my goal to do this so that whenever the conversation came up, I would try to explain that nothing would happen to me, that I was used to traveling alone and talking to people from different countries and with different languages, and that even without understanding the language, I could get by very well with a piece of paper and pencil.

One day after several years of visiting Libya, Osama appeared at the family home and said, "Let's go. I am going to take you to one of the shopping streets that you dream about in the centre of town and "throw you out" and when you've had enough, or any problems, you can call me and I'll come and pick you up right away". He used the words "throw out" because that was the feeling he had on leaving me alone in the middle of the city, as if he were leaving me alone and defenseless and I would not be able to fend for myself.

I knew that they were wrong but I did not want to push, so I said nothing.

Inwardly I was jumping for joy because finally I could go into town with no children or a crowd of people around me. I like people and enjoy being around them but I have to recognize that I needed to be alone and to do exactly what I wanted for me and not

41

in a group. Furthermore, I wanted to see the shops on my own, go where I wanted to, and buy or try on anything I felt like.

Osama and Ibrahim took me by car to the shopping street, "threw me out" after making sure I had my telephone with me and reminding me to call if I had any problems.

It was wonderful. Not only did I have no problems but they treated my beautifully in the shops. They would write down the prices, showed me what I wanted and I had more fun than anybody can imagine. I bought what I felt like without feeling guilty if I left a shop without having bought something. I asked the prices and sizes of a lot of things while just looking until it got late and I called them to come and get me.

I hadn't even hung up the telephone when the car was right on the pavement in front of me. I was surprised as I got into the car.

Later they told me that they were very worried about me and were waiting close by just in case I had any problems. They had been chatting in the car waiting for me on the same street without my knowing.

My return to the family home was a huge event. Everyone was talking surprised at how well I had done, asking me how I had managed and for them it was source of great hilarity when they heard about how I had managed in certain situations in the shops without knowing the language. Osama told me that from now on they would not worry because nothing would happen to me and that they would take me to the shopping areas without his sisters having to go with me.

To all of this, it is important to add that their worries were very basic because Libya is a hospitable and safe country and nobody was worried about my safety or that I would be cheated. Their worries were far more simple like I might feel overwhelmed or not know how to resolve a situation or that there might be some misunderstanding.

In Libya the prices are fixed therefore you do not need to worry about the bargaining in the majority of Arab countries where it makes shopping difficult.

It was very simple because the salespeople do not bother you or follow you around and only would answer me if I asked them something. My questions were simple such as "How much is it?" or asking for a certain size or quantity and then, "Good morning", "thank you" and "good bye".

For a long time and in spite of the fact I went out shopping on my own, they would still take me by car to the shopping areas because I could not find my way.

A few years back I asked them to give me a local map of the area with the idea of going out every day a little further until I could find my way better. I know that it seems silly but the irregular labyrinths we went through by car and by always a different route were difficult for me to remember. I managed my first survey by walking some 20 minutes and reaching a shopping district that I liked a lot. It was after receiving a lot of advice and pleas of not staying out too late so that they would not worry. It was fun, exciting and turned out to be very useful to me because that first outing from the house alone and on foot helped me to get my bearings and I easily began to find my way. The next day I asked for a map to another shopping area and so gradually I was going out more and it was just at this point when I had to leave Libya suddenly as NATO began bombing the country.

What was happening to me in Libya was surprising. I have traveled almost always by myself: by plane, train or car... I have traveled across Spain, visited numerous European or African cities and I have traveled to Libya on my own. Even so, when I finally managed to cross Sabha from one side of the city to another, I was as elated as if I had mastered a great obstacle, as if I had achieved something great in life.

When I talk about going out alone I am always referring to going a long way from the house because right from the start I would go to the corner to buy food or phone cards or to the shops that were nearest to us.

On writing these stories I understand that to some the process of becoming independent might seem slow, however we cannot get away from the family and tribal context in which I was immersed, where each day there were so many visits from entire families or we would do the visiting, or a wedding or some special event. Life flows within the group and each day people organize themselves according to their interests but always within the group and everything fits in following traditions, rules and existing hierarchies.

This meant that my goals of going out shopping were not a priority and there were many other things that interested me and postponed my exploration of the town.

The days would end without my even having had time to call my family.

Each day I spent more time sitting in the main room observing the mothers with their babies and children as much for my work for which I had gone to Libya as out of natural curiosity and pure pleasure. I was surprised at how beautiful the women all were and how they looked after their appearance.

The matriarch of the family had had 15 children in her lifetime yet she was a beautiful, unlined woman. She was warm, well mannered with customs that, at first, seemed submissive to me however later I found out that in that household it was she who was in charge as much of her sons and daughters as her husband. She was, and still is, the most loved and respected woman that I know and with a natural elegance and smile on her lips expressing peace and happiness.

When I saw her come into the room set aside for guests with her tray of small glasses of green tea, I think that what I thought would have been typical of any westerner. Just before coming into the room with a very natural and elegant gesture, she covered her head and then opened the door to the room. She knelt down and served tea to the guests then she got up still smiling and left the room, uncovered her head and continued on with her daily life. My western eyes saw only submissive, feminine behavior in front of the men who were relaxed, laughing and talking in that room. Later I would come to understand that so many people living together in such a small space brought with it certain relationship rules having little to do with hierarchies and submission on which we often comment, without understanding the cause, because in fact, the Libyan women I have known are the ones who rule the roost, supervise the family and, I would say, their husbands too.

In this photo we can see the clothes of the older women in the house and the elegance with which they wear them.

It is not easy to wrap yourself in a piece of fabric like this woman has done, so that her whole body and head are covered, and yet still be able to do the housework with ease. Normally inside the house they do not cover their heads but she covered hers out of coyness when she saw I was taking her picture. She allowed me to take her photograph on one condition: that no stranger would see her face, so I promised her that it would not appear in the picture. I have kept this promise, although to us it may seem a little strange.

The photo also shows "the sofa" and its use. You can see all the things that have accumulated on it and where they really sit. For a westerner it may surprise us to see where this woman is sitting, however, in Libya the sofa would be surprising. I have said it would be surprising because the changes have been too fast, especially since the west invaded the country. Even so, the north of Libya is not the same as the south in the middle of the Sahara where I live.

45

It is also surprising how clean the soles of her feet are if you take into account that they always go barefoot indoors. That is to say, there is no dust or dirt on the floor. However, many of the streets were not paved and so dust is rather normal in the Sahara towns. I remember that in 2011, the year that NATO began bombing, they were starting a project to redo all the city streets and getting all the new houses ready for handing over.

One of the most important differences between the present Libyan houses and those that were on the point of being handed over were the finishes, electrical outlets and switches.

These new houses were no different to our western ones and some even had reverse osmosis filters installed in the kitchens for the water, something that surprised me considering that the water in

Sabha came directly from underground and was very good.

As far as electrical outlets were concerned, this was something that was always tiresome for me because there were very few and I could never find any extension cords so I would have to wait in line to charge the telephone, camera battery or laptop and always keep an eye out for when the outlet was free.

There came a point when I decided to buy an extension cord with 4 outlets - and it was fantastic until it disappeared - because community living has the disadvantage that people take what they need and it would also not have been appropriate to start interrogations as to who had taken it, since I was their guest. Most probably someone needed it at a certain moment and simply took it.

Human nature is basically the same throughout the world and we know that there will always be people who are respectful and others who live their lives taking as much advantage of the energy of others as they can.

The outlets had another very interesting feature and that was that they were all half hanging so that you had to be careful when plugging and unplugging so that you did not end up breaking it. You get used to it, however, and then it becomes second nature.

The same is with the switches which are few and far between and placed haphazardly. For example, in my room where I sleep in the family home there is only one switch next to the door at the height of my face, which means I have to get up to turn off the light at night or, if I want to see something in the middle of the night, I have no choice but to get up to turn on the light. If I go back now, it will be a lot easier as my telephone has a very strong battery.

When I saw these small spotlights which are used to read the screen at night, I thought immediately of Libya and that I would take one when I could go back.

A Visit to Friends

A few days after being in the family home, Osama, my friend and guide, asked me if I would like to go with him to visit a friend because he had to give him something and that way I would get some fresh air since I had spent several days without hardly going out and surrounded by children.

We went to a farm, as they called it, but we would have called it an oasis since it was in the middle of the Libyan Sahara and the only vegetation grew thanks to one or two wells pumping out water.

He got out of the car to go over to his friend who was working while I stayed behind so as not bother them as Osama had told me that he did not speak a word of English. It was the friend, however, who came over to the car to say hello and to invite me the next day to eat at his house with his family. Osama told me that there was no problem, that I should not worry and the only problem that I might have was that nobody spoke English in that family except for one of the sisters, but that they would sort that out. I asked him to come with me since he was his friend but he told me that I had been the one invited and not to worry that I would have a lovely time.

The next day Osama took me to Walit's house, stopped at the door and left me with all the family who only spoke Arabic and not one of the sisters spoke any English. As is normal, they took me to the main living room where all the siblings with their children were arriving and I undertook to "build a relationship" as best I could with them while Walit kept calling me over to his computer, saying "Lio come", and I would go over to the computer where he would show me photos of the family, the desert, the country and also of other Arab countries. Then I would go back to the main room where the rest of the family were waiting, all of us looking at one another and trying to communicate by sign language, through the children, with body language as best we could until the moment came when the food arrived.

A huge tray of pasta and a spoon for dinner, small cucumber salads, as usual fruit on small dishes, various types of juice and water. The fruit was almost always watermelon and I have to say that the Libyan watermelons are the best I have ever eaten. They are delicious and sweet, coming from irrigated areas created out in the desert by the Libyan government where they grow vegetables, melons, watermelons and many other types of fruit which are sold to the Libyans at a nominal price.

One time when I passed close to one of these large cultivated areas, the watermelons were just ripe for eating so we stopped and bought two. Never in my life have I enjoyed a watermelon so much.

Once we had finished our meal, we washed our hands, using the words "come, come" and "go, go", they asked me to accompany one of Walit's sisters to a room and obviously I did so to see what awaited me and always happy to explore new situations.

Walit's sister asked me to undress and I put on the clothes she had laid out for me. I actually had no idea what they expected from me but it was a lot more fun trying on the Libyan clothes than sitting so long in the same living room, so I happily tried on the typical Libyan dress that the women wear today to weddings or for important occasions. When I was dressed, they gave me shoes with the highest heels I have ever worn in my life and then they put the gold jewelry on me that Libyan women usually wear with these clothes. I looked in the mirror and smiled at myself, but before I had time to have a good look, they took me to Walit's mother for her approval.

Not long before, that lady had had a stroke and had lost the ability to speak so her children were teaching her to talk again. I was surprised at the sense of humor with which she faced her own situation, laughing at herself when the words would not come out and we all ended up laughing and they made her repeat the word until it came out right. You felt their great love towards her and, despite her frail condition, she was smiling and very warm.

She rearranged parts of the outfit that she felt were not quite right, gave some instructions which I did not understand, but at that moment another sister appeared with a very intense red lipstick and asked me to put some on. They asked me if I wanted to make up my eyes but I felt that was a little too much since I did not know what they were expecting of me and for me it was just a way of showing me the typical dress, in case I did not know it.

When I was fully dressed and made up, Walit said, "Come, come" and took me outside where he opened the door of the car.

At that moment I felt a little uncomfortable because I had only been in Libya a few days, I was in the house of people I did not know and they were taking me somewhere else, and nobody could explain anything as they spoke zero English or any other language except Arabic. On the other hand, I reminded myself that I was already on the way and if my friends had left me there it was because the trusted these people.

Walit drove the car all over the city while my mind was working overtime. I wondered if I should call Osama and tell him but I realized that I had left my telephone at the house. Finally, Walit stopped the car in front of an Egyptian shop and said, "Come, come". I got down from the car, following him and then finally understood!

They had taken me to an area where they were going to take some photographs in typical Libyan dress, at the same time Walit had made me take my own camera. The photographer told Walit that if he wanted, he could take photographs with his own camera and then others wit

Mine, or perhaps it was Walit who asked the photographer. He was a very nice Egyptian.

Up until then I had always believed I was very shy in front of the camera but clearly this experience relaxed me completely and I simply let myself go while he took photographs. They made me hold a large pitcher in one photo, another was taken seated, another standing, looking this way and that, smiling and in this way they took a lot of pictures while I posed as if I had been doing it all my life. I was laughing inside because I was surprised with myself and was honestly having fun as if I were looking at this situation from afar.

It was a lot of fun finding out what was going to happen next and when. And this is how it was all day.

Once the photo session was over, the Egyptian photographer thanked me and I found out later that he had asked Walit if he could exhibit my photograph. Osama asked me if that was alright and of course I said yes.

Once everything was finished, we took the car back to Walit's house and there I found Osama and Ibrahim waiting and worried about where I had been. They asked me why I had not let them know that I was going out but later everything was fine. On returning to the house a slightly more complicated situation arose in that the sisters wanted me to stay the night. I did not know that this was part of the protocol of Libyan good manners that you had not treated your guest properly unless he had stayed for at least 3 days under your roof so it was perfectly normal for them to request this. The problem was that I did not know this part of Libyan manners and I did not want to openly refuse. If I could have spoken Arabic or they had spoken English or Spanish, then I would have certainly found the words to excuse myself politely. Furthermore, I did not see why these lovely people would want to spend more days with me when they could not even speak to me. Luckily Osama quickly appeared after having greeted the rest of the family while they were "pressuring" me.

He simply said, "Go and change your clothes and we'll be on our way as my older sister is waiting for you because her children want to say goodbye as they are going back home tonight."

Once Osama had said this, they did not carry on insisting I stay and we began our goodbyes.

I forgot one other unexpected thing at Walit's house when I learned something more and this was also a little complicated. I was wearing a necklace of colored beads which one of the little girls in the family had given me. It was a very special present and furthermore I knew that the little girl would be very pleased to see that I always wore it. After being at Walit's house for a short time, one of the sisters who was pregnant asked if I would let her touch the necklace. I gave it to her and she put it around her neck and asked me to give it to her as she liked it very much. I explained to her that it was a present and for this reason I could not give it to her. She insisted, however, laughing that I give it to her and did not return it to me.

I asked her several time as best I could but I thought I could not force the situation any further without knowing what reaction this could provoke being a guest and not being able to express myself in her language.

The truth is I was unhappy that she had not given it back to me and wanted to resolve the situation as best I could but was unable to.

Once I was away from the house and in the car with Osama and Ibrahim, I explained what had happened to me and very calmly and without giving it any importance they explained to me that I should not worry that I would get it back the next day, that it had been perfectly normal because this girl was pregnant and you never denied a pregnant lady anything. Later, once she had time to enjoy the necklace, they would ask Walit to give it back to me. It was at that moment that I began to understand the enormously different attitude, care and respect that everyone had towards pregnant women.

In Libya mothers are revered, especially one's own. In the extreme, some men will not eat the meat of a female animal.

The whole culture and society in general hold mothers in high regard as the most esteemed and important in creation. This attitude towards woman/mother/lover evokes the mystic cults of Isis or the veneration of the cathari and Knights Templar for the figure of Mary Magdalene (wisdom, cosmic union, maternity).

After my first contact with this pregnant lady, I had the opportunity to live in the family home with a sister of Osama who was also pregnant. I watched her a lot because she was pregnant from the top of her head to the tips of her toes. She experienced her pregnancy totally happy and relaxed doing whatever she felt like and because of her condition she was not required to do anything either at work or at home.

I know that this comment might sound strange here where we have so many problems with unjustified work lay-offs, but in Libya the circumstances were very different since most of the population had a government salary without working and in jobs they did not look for the income producing possibilities of an employee, since all the money came from oil and not from the jobs of the other Libyans.

The difference is huge and is not comparable because the quality of life can be much better since nobody's interests are harmed if they contract double the people they need for an office. In this way each one of them has more freedom at their disposal without impacting negatively on their colleagues.

This situation gives rise to a quality of life and freedom that I have never seen before. Libyans do not go to work for five days in order to attend a wedding, or three days to go to a funeral or for multiple reasons relating to family or tribal obligations without the "company" becoming resentful. Quite the contrary, the bosses understand perfectly amongst other reasons because the do the same when necessary. It is simply that in Libyan culture and to the government of Jamahiriyah, looking after the family and family and social wellbeing are as important, or more important, than working.

An even clearer example came about, some time afterwards, when the husband of this girl who was pregnant, Osama's sister, had a blood clot. Her boss at the office told her to only come to work when she could because he understood perfectly that, in her condition, with small children and a husband, it would be very hard for her to come to the office. She would go for several hours on the day that she could because she really was going through a bad time in spite of the help from the family.

To understand this more clearly, we have to change the way of thinking we have in the west because, to begin with, the Libyans obtain money from the oil and not from working in the town. There was as much money as needed and nobody felt the need to command a salary without working but rather the opposite. They consider that the oil belongs to all Libyans and everyone has a right to benefit from it. (At least, it is like that in the Jamahiriyah Libya that I knew). For them it was as important to go to work as it was to attend to tribal or family obligations, or perhaps I should say the family or tribe were more important to them than a job outside of the home because it comes into the realm of social values.

A man will be valued more socially the better his family live. By the same token, a woman is valued in her family environment for her motherhood and behavior. This does not mean, however, that they do not value university studies or their jobs.

I hope that my comments are not interpreted with Western bias. These values are not unique so much so that the majority of the women living in the same house as me had studied at university.

In Libya school is compulsory and free, including books and school materials. University was also free. There are schools in all the cities and towns in Libya from north to south, east to west. Furthermore, there were universities in all Libyan cities with a minimum of 75,000 inhabitants.

Boys as well as girls attended university and had the same aspirations and opportunities to study.

When a person has dedicated so many years to his education, whether a man or a woman, they will value their profession much more than another who works only to get by and possibly will have a set of different values. For example, in the first family with which I lived, the father had been doing a postgraduate degree in England. While they were staying in this country, his wife had six children and did not work. However, that woman was a teacher of Arabic and as soon as her youngest daughter started school, she went back to work in her profession.

The women were not worried because they received a monthly maternity payment from the government and then they also knew they could buy basic food products in the state department stores so that, with all this in addition to the husbands basic wage, they were living well. Then no matter how little enterprising the husband might be, there were hundreds of way of working and making money to improve your quality of life.

Weddings and their Invitations

Weddings were another source of wonderful experiences and surprises for me.

Shortly after arriving in Libya, I began to hear comments about the upcoming marriage of Omar, the younger brother of Osama. They told me that I was invited and that they hoped I would come back to Libya for it.

On asking when the wedding was going to be, they replied, "next year at the beginning of the year". So, I began to get excited thinking about my next visit, that I would buy some new clothes for my first Libyan wedding, about the present I would give to the couple and in organizing my life in order to be able to return for the wedding.

It seemed important to pin down the date, not just for my own personal planning purposes, but also it seemed obvious to me that planning a wedding nowadays requires a lot of forward organization and it was logical to start from an exact date. I know this from my daughter's wedding which she began to organize a year before in order to reserve a date for the Church, choose a place for the reception, the menu, the bridal dress, the music, invitations and so many other things, so I assumed that they already knew the date. However, they never said anything more concrete other than "In a few months, at the beginning of the year". After asking several different people several times and seeing that nobody told me the same date except "more or less", I began to wonder if they were being evasive because they did not want me to come to the wedding.

However, one day the matriarch of the house reminded me that she would be very pleased if I went to her son's wedding. My friend, Osama, also told me that the whole family would be delighted if I could go to his brother's wedding... which would be in the summer. "In the summer? But hadn't they been saying at the beginning of the year?"

So, I asked the date again and they said that probably it would be before Ramadan in July or August.

How could it be that they kept changing the date and, being something so imminent, nobody knew the exact date? I tried talking about it to my friend, Mannar, who explained smiling, as always, that it would be in the summer for sure, in July or August. In spite of my western mentality, I understood that making comparisons is always negative and depending on what sort of questions I could pose about their ways, this was something I had to avoid at all costs like never judging their behavior or customs.

For this reason, I kept on asking every now and again if they already knew the date of the wedding, however, I never received any exact information.

One day, unexpectedly and now almost summertime, I cannot remember if it was June or thereabouts, they calmly told me as if the most normal thing in the world, that the wedding would be the first week in September but that the preparations would begin some two weeks earlier because the whole family had a lot to do.

I replied that I would like very much to help with the preparations and for them to tell me when they were going to start and when I could go.

My friend, Osama, told me that of course I was invited to stay at his house whenever I wanted but that I needed to understand that during the preparations for a wedding, the whole family works a lot and they are all very nervous. It was important for me to know that the attention they would be able to give to me would not be the same.

I was in Libya two weeks before the wedding. For starters, in Libya the bridegroom and his family are responsible for all the work and payment of the wedding while the bride dedicates herself to making herself beautiful for that date, at least that is what it seems on the face of it, because when you actually know the couple, you understand that they talk to each other every day and work as a team.

I am going to explain this wedding seen from outside, since I did not know the bride until the day she got married, however, I know that they fell in love at work because both worked at the hospital. Afterwards his family, that is my family, which means the matriarch of the family, was against the marriage because she wanted her son to marry someone closer and of the same tribe. However, as always happens in these cases, love and perseverance won the day and finally they acquiesced to go to her house and ask for her hand.

From this moment on they were engaged and he began to look

58

for a place to live, furnish it and decorate it just for her, to save for the reception that would last for 5 days between the bride's house and that of the bridegroom, buy two camels for the reception, one for the bride's family and one for his own, buy gold that the bride's tribe receives because this gold will be for the bride which will be held as her life insurance. These bridal jewels are very typical and enormous!

Of course, they depend also on the financial standing of the bridegroom's family. If they are very poor, they will buy them in silver with a gold finish. What the brides receive is a real fortune in gold.

This jewelry will be given to the bride on one of the days of the wedding and she will wear them when she goes to another wedding or on special occasions including gold necklaces that are so long they hang to the waist. In this photograph there is only some of the jewelry because there are also many large rings for each finger plus bracelets and chokers.

The bridegroom's family also will buy all sorts of perfumes

and scents so that the bride can get ready for the wedding with face masks, perfumes for when she marries, henna for her body so that she will be more pleasing to the husband.

They fill different baskets for the wedding with everything the bride might need or want. And not only for the wedding, but also for after the wedding for her own personal hygiene and beauty.

Then they buy a trousseau which they put in special baskets for the brides: dresses, bags, shoes, underwear etc.

These baskets are always pink and are sold in special shops where you can buy all kinds of things for weddings.

The day before the wedding, I saw that they were sending invitations and I was more than surprised until I realized that, to them, it was not really an invitation but more a confirmation that tomorrow the wedding would begin and as a reminder, in an attempt to imitate weddings seen on western television shows.

On the one hand all the preparations are based on Libyan culture and will vary a little from tribe to tribe and then they add small western innovations like the European dress, the bride's wedding dress or the photograph of the bride and bridegroom. They never used to take photographs in Libya however now it is traditional for the bride and groom to go to a studio and have THE PHOTO taken.

The bride is going to use 5 outfits which she will also receive with the trousseau from the groom. The wedding outfits are made from special natural striped silk fabrics which come in ALL shades and colors matching shoes and handbags and an upper part which will peek out a little from beneath the fabric. The bride will receive one in white, one in pink and then others, depending on the tribe and the taste of the groom's sisters, who will buy one or another.

At the weddings that I have attended, the bride wears a western style bridal dress, on the day that she invites her family to  her home and they hire a large type of throne where she will sit while the extended family come to offer their congratulations.

In the evening we also went to greet several members of the family of the future husband. On this occasion, I had the honor to be invited.

This photograph shows the bride on the day she went to the husband's home to be united in matrimony and then on to their new home together. First of all, she is given a beauty treatment on her skin, perfumed and then she dresses in another wedding outfit with some of the gold jewelry given to her by the husband.

I   would love to have taken photographs of all the ceremonies and proceedings over the 5 days of the wedding, however, most Libyans do not like photographs, especially those taken by a stranger because they do not know how they will be used.

The future husband and wife gave me permission to take all the photographs I wanted, but I encountered opposition from several members of the family so I could only take a few.

Libyan ceremonies are huge as all members of the tribe attend, although not all can stay for the entire time.

It is surprising how people will come from the other side of the country to attend a relative's wedding, even having had very little advance notice.

I was also surprised to see that most of the guests did not bring gifts for the bride and groom because there is no "obligation" to do so, like in the west. What is, however, normal is that the closest family members help as much as they can with the preparations for the banquet either in buying food, fixing up the future house of the newlyweds or erecting the huge tent for the wedding.

The Day I brought a Wedding to a Halt

One of the most joyful and lovely ceremonies is when the women in the family all dressed in their party dresses in the same style of the bride but in other colours, take out the trousseau that they are going to take to the bride while they sing, dance, beat a drum on the ground. This was a magical moment that I could not help photographing. Flassss! My flash went off.

It was a very special occasion that I watched for a long time completely enthralled by such a unique demonstration of beauty and joy that I shall never forget.

The women were seated enjoying everything while there was a large drum on the ground that two women were beating.

One woman took her head scarf and wrapped it around her hips and began to dance sensually, full of rhythm and gaiety. After a few minutes, she handed the scarf to another woman who repeated the same thing but with her own personal style of dancing.

That huge room full of color and music was so lovely that I wanted to immortalize it in a photograph, even though, deep down, I suspected that some might not like it. I pressed the button and did not realize the effect the flash would have on a dimly lit room.

As the flash went off...

Everything suddenly came to a standstill. The drums stopped beating, the women stopped dancing and there was a penetrating silence in the room. I was petrified because everyone was looking at me! I had broken the enchantment by trying to capture the moment. Then my friend came up to me and asked me not to take any photographs because some of the women had complained.

I felt that I had been disrespectful and had ruined the party, however, it was very hard not to be able to photograph those ceremonies so modern yet, at the same time, so ancestral because I intuitively felt that they were going to disappear soon and could only be remembered by those who had experienced them.

In fact, in the north of Libya many couples get married in one day like in the west because all these ceremonies are costly and require a lot of effort. In the south they still continue with part of the ceremonies but have reduced the weddings to a maximum of two or three days.

The cars that take the newlyweds to their evening wedding and then to their home are very picturesque. There are companies who specialize in painting and decorating them for the occasion.

The Wedding and its Different Stages

The different stages and details of a wedding vary according to tribe and region of Libya but there are a series of steps that are essential to follow to observe cultural protocol. If, for example, we follow the general steps of a wedding in the Tripolitania region, they would be:

1. The Proposal or Khitba

Since in the past the boy and girl did not know one another nor had had any contact, the young man did not have the opportunity to get to know his future bride or choose her or propose to her. This was something that was left to the parents.

Directly or indirectly, mothers know their sons' tastes and armed with all this knowledge and experience, would visit and find the best way to get to know possible young female candidates for their son, asking for assistance from close relatives and neighbours until finding the appropriate woman. Once the choice has been made and after having received the approval from father and his son, then a delegation of women made up of close relatives of the boy go to the girl's house. They have previously arranged a meeting with her mother.

The delegation is received by the girl's family and in a celebratory atmosphere laid on for the occasion, the boy's family formally ask for her hand.

Once the family has accepted, they set a date for the engagement. During the meeting they agree the conditions for the celebrations in both families.

2. Normally once the Khitba has been finalized, the girl's family have a small party in which the women dress in their finest clothes and jewels. The future bride is in charge of receiving the guests and is congratulated by everyone. This party gives the bride the chance for her future mother-in-law to get to know her better, see how she cooks, moves, dresses, how she gets on with others, etc. If all goes well and no problems arise, after several days they will celebrate a similar party at the home of the groom.

3. The future groom attends with his father, accompanied by close family members and his closest friends who will get to know the father of the bride and in this way they will get to know each other better.

At the end of these two parties, the engagement is reaffirmed if all has gone well. Normally many discussions arise lasting hours which are generally on the subject of finances. They discuss what they are going to give the couple and whether they will give money or assets and several other finer points, normally of a financial nature. They also discuss where the couple are going to live.

If the two parties, including the discussions, end on a positive note and the relationship is not broken off, then they set an approximate date for the wedding.

This is a basic step based on old Libyan culture, however, nowadays many young people meet at university, or at work or at a friend's house, fall in love and when they decide to marry they follow all the above protocol.

I have a friend married to a delightful woman and they are both very happy. I asked him how he had married and where he had met his wife. His reply was that he had placed all his trust in the person who knows him best and loves him most, his mother. That is to say that this young man who was born in the seventies on his own volition had left the choice of his wife in his mother's hands.

I also know others who have known each other at university, others at work etc. And, in the end, I have seen that it is like in the west but following a different ritual within a different culture.

The magic of Libya is precisely that the enormous changes it has undergone over the past few generations thanks to education and the spectacular increase in the standard of living, have all been made while remaining respectful of its old customs and culture.

This fusion of old and new produces a result that you can only come to understand by immersing yourself completely, since most things are not what they seem at first sight to the western eye.

2. The Engagement or "Bayan"

Celebrations of the nuptials take place simultaneously in both families of the future bride and groom. The closest relatives to the couple are invited to the bride's family home and in her presence both sets of parents announce the plans for the wedding.

Of course, the future bride has already been told by her mother and she has the right to refuse if she so wishes.

The mother acts as if she has not met the future groom or informed her about his age, character, family, social position etc. and that her daughter has already told her mother that she agrees to the marriage. Even so, the bride must give her approval in front of both families of the couple.

Once she has said yes before both families, they then recite a chapter from the Koran "Fatiha" and the engagement is finalized.

At the same time, a similar ceremony takes place with the future bridegroom in the mosque or another public place. The girl must accept the engagement in front of the groom as well and then the union is officially concluded.

The couple, however, will not be married until the wedding takes place. The engagement is registered by a judge or notary.

When the wedding is set for a long time afterwards, then a date will be fixed for a new meeting to continue the negotiations. This celebration would be comparable to an engagement party in the west.

Normally during these parties, the groom's family, when they go to the bride's house, take several baskets for the wedding with gifts for the bride as well as perfume, sweets, henna and food which will generally be eaten during the celebrations.

These gifts will vary depending on the families and their finances but independently of everything, they must include jewellery (at least one piece) and dresses that the bride will wear during the ceremony.

When the groom's family arrive, they will be received with typical Arab "yuyus"[1] and many times the young girls in the family and the bride's friends will dance with drums. In this joyful yet simple ceremony, the engagement is sealed.

The families return to their homes, tell the news, and this will be the topic of conversation between relatives and friends and before long will reach the tribes of the couple.

During the days, weeks or months until the couple marry, the future bridegroom will send presents to his fiancée, normally clothes and jewelry, with his mother who sometimes will be accompanied by close family and friends.

3. The Wedding or "Dakha"

Several months or even a year later, the wedding will be celebrated.

The union between the couple takes place on a Friday or Monday night because, according to Arab superstition, these are the most auspicious days for a better future for the couple.

All during the week before the happy wedding night, the families are busy with the preparations for the celebrations and at sunset on D-day, the bride is led into the arms of her husband. The husband takes her to their bedroom where the marriage is consummated.

In theory and practice, the union is now sealed and consummated.

Nowadays several couples go to a hotel, as is fashionable in the movies, or they go to their new home and afterwards take a trip as in western tradition. For several days afterwards there are postnuptial parties and, when all is over, everything goes back to normal, except that now a new family has been born.

The chronological order of the celebrations would be:

Thursday: Al Mustadhnat which is the plural of "mustadha" which means "inviters". The name itself says it all and consists in two or three women who act as invitations in the west. These go to the homes of friends and family and invite them to the happy event. These women usually arrive at the future groom's house the day before and spend the Wednesday night singing and dancing and playing instruments such as the "Darbuka" in the presence of the groom and his neighbors.

The next day they dress in their best clothes and perfumes, receive gifts in thanks for what they are doing, and leave the groom's house to first go to the house of the future bride because she is the first that must be invited. From there, they will go from house to house inviting on behalf of the mother of the bride or groom, depending on whom they are inviting, and in each house the inviters are received with yuyus, drinks, sweets and even sometimes money.

Friday: This is also dedicated to inviting everyone and in the evening, on arriving back at the house, the day ends with singing and dancing.

Saturday: "Yaum ar-Ra" which means "Day of Rest". However, the rest is relative because this day is dedicated to cleaning the house from top to bottom and to finishing all the preparations for the wedding and last minute purchases.

Sunday: This is the fourth day and has two names, Yaum al halu or the day of the cakes because this is the day dedicated to making elaborate pastries for the wedding. These pastries are quite different from those in the west. They are eastern specialities and several are even specialities of the region itself.

Some of the best known specialities are:

Baclawa which consists of thin layers of pastry filled with almond paste, sugar and then covered with honey.

Magrudh: small pieces of semolina dough, oil and sugar baked in the oven and sometimes these pieces are filled with a paste made from dates and then soaked in honey.

Gharaiba: This is also a mix of semolina, butter and sugar but in the shape of a cone.

Kaak: They use the same ingredients as above but in different proportions so that the cake is harder, also the shape changes and is now round.

Dibla: Small sheets of flour dough, fried and rolled in honey while hot.

There are many other types of pastries for this day but these are the best known and the most popular.

We have said that this fourth day has two names and up until now I have described the women's day.

For the men it is Nahar al Qila or the day of the curtain. Certainly the name is curious and in order to explain its meaning, a small description of the architecture of a Libyan house is in order. They have a large, long porch which gives on to a big patio which is more or less square with a marble or cement floor. Doors from different rooms open on to the patio.

This patio is around 100 sq metres and is where the wedding celebrations take place. Even though in Libya there is no need to worry about rain or cold as in the west, the patios are covered with large pieces of canvas to keep out the sun or wind or any rain that could bother the guests and so they can dance, eat and enjoy themselves without any worries.

The fourth day the friends of the groom go and buy a huge piece of fabric which will cover the patio and they take it to the house by the longest route through neighbouring streets followed by friends and relatives singing to the beat of drums. This musical gathering is called a "nuba". And so the "curtain" which has arrived with so much fanfare is then placed over the patio while the "nuba" keeps on singing.

Monday: This is a day that is full of activity.
It is the day of the bath.
In the morning the bride, together with two attendants and escorted by friends will go to the public baths, normally rented and reserved just for her. Nowadays, this is done at home and is called the "nuptial bath" which the ancient Greeks and Romans also took. Irregardless of its origin and place where it is taken, the bride spends the whole day bathing and afterwards puts on the pink dress, pink being the colour that symbolizes virginity.

While the bride and her friends are in the bathroom, the "zimzamat" (female orchestra) are singing and dancing to entertain the guests. Those invited wear their best clothes and most sumptuous jewels. They sit savouring the refreshments whilst listening to the songs of the zimzamat.

This day is also called the Day of Exchange or "Al Tawid" or Al Lawda" because early in the morning the older women from the groom's home go to the bride's house to ask for an exchange. The closest relatives dress the bride in typical traditional dress, with much jewelry and they cover her, including her face which will be covered with a veil that will also be used on her wedding night. They will then guide her to the covered patio of the house where the guests are still seated listening to the music of the zimzamat.

When the bride arrives, two women who are not divorcees approach the bride and make her circle seven times around a basket placed on two cushions and full of henna. It goes without saying that the cushions and basket for the occasion are special and covered in tulle with silver embroidery.

While the bride circles around the basket, another woman follows her with a mirror. When she has finished, the bride will sit down and stand up seven times from the basket. After looking in the mirror, the bride will join the women in the "zighrit" and all the women will "yuuuuuyuuuu".

When I asked the women why the bride circles around and looks in the mirror and they all sing "yuuuuyuuuu", they replied that it was so that fortune and good luck will be with her at all times and that she might have a bright future.

It is now the fifth day and the festivities continue in the groom's house where they call this day "Nahar al guffa" which means "The Day of the Basket". This basket is very important because the whole family has spent the day preparing it, or rather its contents. The basket is specially made for the occasion from palm leaves and artistically covered in silk and embroidered in silver. It must be very beautiful since it contains special and precious gifts which they will take to the bride as her wedding gift. It is very rare, however, that it is just one basket. There is also a basket full of beauty treatments for the bride such as perfume, henna, face and body masks etc.

After a meal, these baskets together with a group of women go to the bride's house in a procession of cars. A band comprising a clarinet and drums will go in the first car. This is the "nuba" which I have already mentioned.

Nowadays, these convoys of cars go along honking their horns and some even fire shots into the air. The whole city hears the bridal party from the deafening noise they make.

The shots are something new from the Libyan crisis since weapons are sold in the street at very low prices to the point that "companies" now rent them of every calibre to make a noise at weddings. It is one more sign of the pacific nature of the Libyans that on seeing weapons, they give them a practical use at the festivities rather than using them for destructive purposes.

A friend told me that, with the new situation in Libya, because he lived on a farm he felt the need for a weapon to defend himself against armed gangs who might want to rob him. However, the first time a gang came to rob him, he had no ammunition.

I was surprised that he would keep a weapon without any ammunition in such a dangerous place but he commented that he had bought a box of ammunition but, since they had nothing to eat, he had gone out into the desert to hunt rabbits. It appears that he wasted a lot of the ammunition because he was not a good shot unless the rabbit was right in front of a dune, so the bullet would end up embedded in the sand.

In the old days, these processions or caravans would be on foot, but for a long time now they have been made by car. Among many of the reasons is that people are now living much further apart and sometimes must travel 80 km to reach the bride's house.

Upon the arrival of the procession at the bride's house, it is greeted with "yuuuuyuuus". Then there is a little time to rest, have a refreshing drink, eat pastries and chat for bit.

Tuesday: Nahar ar-Rabi or The Day of Spring. It is given this name because it is the day that the flowers take centre stage.

What type of flowers? These are of the human kind. It is the young girls as old as 10 decked out in the clothing and hairdos of the older women, creating a pretty spring-like display of color.

Early in the afternoon, when the girls are already busy and taking their places and the Zimzamat is singing and beating their drums, a woman sits on a huge white sheet and with great care and skill, will take out all the gifts from the groom from the baskets, one by one until they are completely empty. Most will be used to make the bride beautiful since most are henna, perfume, incense...

The contents of the basket called "guffa" or "alaqa" or "birti" are, (using the names that have been given to me):

Henna, Myrtle, Cloves, Cherry stones, Walnut bark, Sweet Marjoram, Lavender, Dried roses, Orris root, Antomony (Kohl), Benzoin, Incense, Aromatic Wood, Caio Boya, Resin, Musk, Gum Amoniac, Fasuk, Assafoetid, Alum, Saffron, Cumin, Anis, Fennel, Love-in-a-Mist, Irepidium, Sativum, Iron Sulphate, Copper Sulphate, Aloes, Myrrh, Sugar Candy, Chick Pea Flour, sweetmeats, comb, mirror, thread, bars of soap, needles, eye pencil.

Of course, this will vary considerably from one district to another in Libya and even within Tripoli itself.

The basket is opened in front of the girls who are seated next to the white sheet. The woman who is taking all the articles from the baskets must take a minimum quantity from each of them and rub them on the sole of the right foot of one of the girls. This custom ensures "breaking the liver" (of the future groom) which to Libyan women means being able to handle the husband, being humble, knowing how to advise him, take care of him and put into words what he likes.

Returning to the ceremony: Once the baskets have all been emptied and everything placed on the sheet, we come to the second phase of the ceremony which consists of pounding the henna.

In reality, nowadays, henna is sold in powdered form in ready to use bags. However, in the past it had to be prepared. Henna is a herb which is bought dried and must be pulverized into a paste which the women then apply as a dye on their hands and feet.

The bride places herself in front of the mortar as if she were going to pound the henna and she sits as tradition dictates, with the right leg extended and the left crossed.

Then a woman will come to her with two threads of red silk. The bride will tie the first around her left knee and the second she will wind around her face above the mouth and tie at the back of the neck, after placing a little sugar under her tongue.

Next she puts the bride's khulkhal (a silver and gold bracelet which is worn around the ankle) over the mortar. The bride then begins the ceremony by starting to grind the henna three or four times and then hands over to other girls who will pound the herb. However, before this, they remove the read threads from around her knee and mouth and these are cut into small pieces over the heads of the girls so that they will marry as soon as possible. These girls are also busy with another occupation or superstition that involves rubbing their legs against those of women who have already married. They tell them: "Hukki saqui ala saqik w-illi saqni saqak"which means "Rub your leg against mine and everything that has guided me will guide you too".

Each one of these things always has a meaning.

The thread around the mouth with the sugar under the tongue signifies that in her new home and future life, the bride will not be a gossip and when she speaks, her words will always be sweet like the sugar under her tongue. The second thread that the she wears around her knee comes from the camels and means that they hope the bride will be at one with her home, close to her home and that she will never leave it, because she feels comfortable and settled.

It goes without saying that, during the whole of this day the "zimzamat" has not stopped playing and singing while refreshments and pastries are offered to the girls who are the protagonists on this "Day of Spring".

The supper will be special both in the homes of the bride and groom and they will eat couscous with Usban. (This is a piece of lamb filled with the heart, liver and lungs of the lamb and cooked in couscous soup).

A new figure now appears on the scene and this is the "Zayana" who will be the hairdresser or, nowadays, beautician. This lady will supervise all that concerns the make-up and hair of the bride.

Henna is one of the most important things in the makeup of the bride. After the sun sets, the bride will dissolve the henna until it forms a paste perfect for dying her hands and feet and those of her attendants. Once this paste is ready, the bride leaves it on a large tray in the form of a cone and introduces a number of candles and eggs.

All this is done in front of the guests and zimzamat, which continues singing, but now they do it standing so that the bride's fortune will always be good.

Those making up the zimzamat, the relatives and all present afterwards will enjoy the delicious couscous, pastries, drinks and a rest after such a busy day. The rest, however, will not mean that the day has finished.

On the Tuesday evening the "laylat al-henna as saghira" will be celebrated. This means "Henna Night". As you can imagine, this is the night that the bride's hands and feet will be dyed, as well as those of the women present, using the henna that has been prepared a few hours earlier.

Late in the evening, the bride is taken very slowly by the zayana to the place where the henna will be applied. At the same time the drums beat and the zimzamat continues to sing accompanied by the yuuuuuyuuus of all the women there.

Before they start, all the women present at the ceremony will give a certain sum of money called "ramu" which is a contribution towards expenses and normally this money is given to the Zayana because it is understood that she will not charge for her services. The saying goes that the greater the money, the greater the level of friendship between the bride or family. As soon as the "ramu" has been done, the bride will stretch herself out on the floor on comfortably placed cushions and the women will apply the henna while those around will sing a traditional song especially for this occasion.

A great part of the evening is taken up with the henna and the rest of the night they keep singing, dancing and preparing for the wedding.

Wednesday: Lailat al henna al kabira or Henna Night. The preparations come to their most intense point since the great day is rapidly approaching. The hustle and bustle increases as do the nerves and both families are very busy.

The Zayana returns to the groom's home to burn "zlizia" for all the guests. It will also be her job to dress the hair of all the members of the family and then the guests. Afterwards they put on their makeup to then go to the bride's house in a procession preceded by two bands: "la nuba" and "zimzamat".

When they arrive, t hey will be received with all the honours and offered drinks and pastries to the yuuuuuyuuus of the women.

As soon as the ceremony of protocol has finished, the bride comes out of her room, the mother or sister of the bride give her a gift which is generally a ring or a bracelet or gold medallion. Then the bride gives money to those forming the "zimzamat" and "zayana". Then the application of henna begins again as the night before accompanied by music and singing.

Thursday "Laylat ad Dakhla" or "Wedding Night". Finally, the great night arrives while everything is a race, telephone calls, preparations etc. and fraying nerves from both families in a total whirlwind of confusion.

The groom, accompanied by his closest friends, will go to the public baths for a bath and massage. Although, nowadays, in most part of Libya they take a bath at home or a shower because of the scarcity of water. I have never seen anyone fill up a bath in Libya and the public baths are not as common as in Turkey. For this reason, the day of the bath has lost a lot of its symbolism with many friends.

Throughout the celebrations the groom will be called "Sultan" and a "Minister to the Sultan", who must be a married man, will be appointed. The Minister must advise him on everything he has to do, the customs that must be respected, the traditions that must be observed.

In the afternoon both parties finalize the marriage contract together with the legal representatives of the couple, the guests and the judge. Then the first chapter of the Koran: Fatiha is read. Afterwards, refreshments and sweets are served.

As far as the woman is concerned, the day starts with "Ash Shadir" which consists of applying essential oils on her body and on the henna to give it a brighter colour. Then in the afternoon the bride will sit on large cushions and her hair will be skilfully and patiently brushed. It is important to remember that the girls never cut their hair and for this reason it is normally waist length. The hair style is decorated with silver ornaments and even gold coins.

Once her hair has been done, the bride will take off the pink dress and finally put on the wedding dress.

The guests of the groom will form a procession and together with the Zimzamat will go to the bride's house to the beat of the drums and there they will join up with the guests from the bride's house and the bride herself. Now they will all go to the new home of the groom which will be the home of the newlyweds. When they come to the future house of the bride and groom, the bride is given a pot of water, a key and an egg which had been dyed with henna the day before. The water symbolizes peace, the key expresses the desire that the first born be a son and the egg symbolizes life and harmony.

With these three symbols the bride crosses the threshold of her house and when she reaches the door of the bedroom, with her right hand she will break an egg by banging it on the door. This act signifies that her presence and harmony will spread throughout the family. She then enters the bedroom with all the members of her husband's family and they exchange spoonfuls of sweets made especially for the occasion so that in the future they might be sweet to one another. Then she will wait for the arrival of the new husband.

The groom has been in the mosque with his Minister and friends. Afterwards they leave to go to the house in procession. The groom walks with his minister on the right who talks to him all the time giving him advice or simply telling jokes to relieve the tension.

When the groom and his entourage arrive at the house, they read the first chapter of the Koran once more. Then the groom goes into the house and to the room where his new wife awaits.

On arriving at the bedroom he will find five women at the door holding candles. Then one of the women brings him the pot full of water. He will break it at the same time the youuuuuuus are heard from everywhere. The groom goes into the room and there the zazaya, standing next to the bride, will give a very sweet drink from the same glass to the newlyweds. Next, the groom will cross her palm with money and will close the door.

Friday: Nahar al-Mahdhir

As evening falls there is a huge party for everyone that will go on all night after the bridegroom has gone to the bedroom. He will not return until the next day accompanied by the bride.

Everything returns to normal and life goes on as before.

Henna

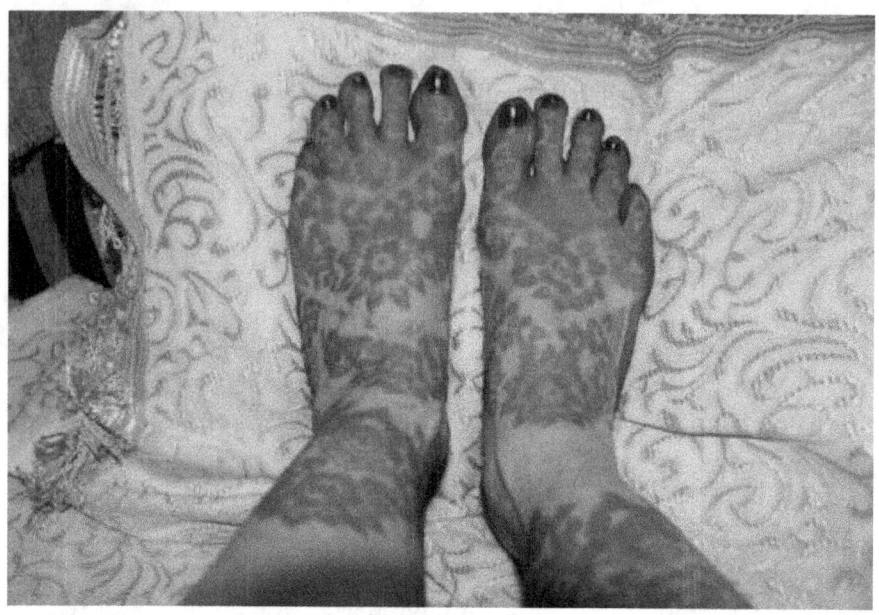

Decorating the body with brown henna is a very important practice to Libyan women and much appreciated by the men.

The word "henna" comes from Hannan which means, kind, tender, loving.

Unmarried women never paint themselves with henna.

Before the marriage, the family of the bride decorate her entire body with brown henna. It is a long and laborious process.

They buy stencils with all sorts of different designs and each woman spends a lot of time choosing which designs she likes and each one is made to fit on a part of the body. They even decorate the soles of the feet.

They carefully place the stencils on the skin and secure them with a sort of adhesive strip. Next, they paint on the henna made with several secret family ingredients so that it shines more or lasts longer or to slightly change the colour etc. Then they cover the area with silver foil or plastic film and then plastic bags. You cannot move for at least six hours so that the painting is perfect. For this reason it is important to take care of any basic needs before embarking on the process.

Once the minimum amount of time has elapsed, they remove the henna and the stencils then cover the painted areas with oil and they leave them for a few hours more to refresh the colour and fix it.

The next day they take a shower to get rid of any remains of the henna and then it is ready. It will last for about a month, depending on how much soap is used and the type of skin.

The bride will always have her hands and feet painted for the first year of marriage until she has her first child.

Every Libyan woman will put henna on her hands and feet when she has to attend a wedding or other important occasion.

People's taste and feelings according to their different cultures are surprising. By this, I mean it all depends on their experiences throughout their childhood.

According to my Libyan friends, a woman painted with henna has a certain appeal and for this reason, two days before returning to Spain with my family, they treated me to having my hands, feet and legs painted with henna so that my husband would be pleased. They would not stop talking about how pleased he would be and how surprised. They never stopped telling me that my husband would be delighted and that he would be very surprised.

Observing their faces and comments, I realized that it never crossed their minds that my husband might not like it, and that was exactly what I was thinking would happen, but I held back from telling them. And that's exactly what happened. When I got home my husband asked me what I had on my hands and then asked me to take it off. Then he asked me how long it would take to wear off and not once did he make a positive comment about it.

I must say that when I am in Libya I feel very comfortable and I actually enjoy painting myself with henna. When I get back to Spain I feel a little uneasy and notice that it's not the same. It is difficult to go to work or to a formal place with your hands completely painted with henna. People look at you strangely and want you to explain all about it.

To them, henna is something they find sexually attractive and it is a way for the woman to make herself beautiful, just like we use makeup and dye our hair or the many other things we do to make ourselves more attractive. The young girls dream of wearing henna when they are older and they take the leftover henna and paint their hands with it.

Each woman creates her own style for painting her hands because it will be something that she will do very often.

The Libyan girls take good care of themselves and are very vain as well as sensual. Normally they use the days when they are menstruating to get together with their sisters and to help each other make themselves beautiful.

In the family home where I was staying, each sister had a speciality and all the others would go to her for sprucing up.

One would practise threading to remove hair from the faces of her sisters and sister-in-law with a technique that I found astounding. As they are dark haired, any hair that grows is noticeable so they remove it from the entire face.

It is also true that the light in the Sahara is so bright that any hair or mark on the skin is doubly more noticeable, and I say this from my own experience, so I understood all this right away.

They remove the hair from the entire body, including the intimate areas. Sometimes they use a shaver or hair remover like Epi-Lady or some women use a sugar paste which is very much like cold wax.

Recipe for the Libyan Hair Removing Paste

2 cups of sugar
2 cups of water
Juice of half a lemon

Heat all the ingredients in a pot until they begin to boil and the mixture begins to turn golden. Then, turn off the heat and allow to cool.

Once cold they take a piece of the mixture in their hands knead it like dough and then it is ready to be used in the same way as cold wax.

They all have long hair and use natural masks to condition it and then they dress it in some wonderful styles.

They love to use makeup, especially for the eyes with many colors that match with the clothing they are wearing. The final result is a work of art.

Jewelry

All married Libyan women have jewelry which is their pride and joy as well as their security and they show it off every chance they get.

It is different to ours and their taste when choosing it bears no resemblance to ours.

I Expect and admire their jewelry, however, I have never managed to buy a piece of Libyan jewelry because they do not fit in with my style and I cannot see them on me, except in the above photograph in which the matriarch of the family allowed me to wear her jewelry and then I returned each piece to its special box.

These necklaces of large medallions which reach almost to the waist is the piece of jewelry most married women have and you can see it on show in all of the Libyan jewelry shops.

Each family distinguishes its economic status by the quantity and quality of these pieces because, although they may all look the same, the thickness of the gold plate varies a great deal, as does the weight.

They are sold by weight in the jewelry stores so that instead of looking at the price of the piece of jewelry, we look at the weight. The reason for this is that, at weddings, it is customary for the tribe or family to give a determined weight of gold in jewelry as a gift.

Gold is highly valued, however, they do not place a great deal of importance on precious stones.

According to their rules, the tribes know the weight of gold that they should give to the bride.

The Barber

Not only the women remove the hair from their faces. The truth is that in Libya you never see men with large eyebrows or hairs growing around the eyebrows or in the ears or nose. However, I never had time to ask myself why this was until some of my friends came to Sabha and decided to go to the barber. They went into the barber shop and were asked if they wanted "the works". My friends, all happy and relaxed and feeling at home in that atmosphere which they really did not know, agreed to everything.

The barber began with a deep cleansing of the skin and then with thread removed the excess hair around the eyebrows and eyes until he got to the beard. The beard is shaved the same as in the west.

The first of my friends told me that when he was having his hair removed, his eyes were watering and he was seeing stars because he had never in his life had that hair removed before, but he did not want to show any pain so that the other friend would have it done too and see stars like him. When he was telling us this, I remember that we laughed a lot but I have to say that his face looked much better and appeared much cleaner. It was then that I realized that the Libyans' faces all looked clean and now I knew the reason.

Who would imagine that the Libyan men were so vain? I had heard my Libyan friends mention how they were going to the barber, but it had never crossed my mind what that actually meant.

Osama commented that they were used to the hair removal and that it never hurt. He was surprised that western men did not do it.

I understood that he never would have commented on it because it is something natural to his culture and would not have remotely considered that outside of Libya it was not something normal. Once you know this and look at the photograph on the left, for example, it is clearly noticeable that the eyebrows are thinner and the area around the eyes is clean, compared to the photograph on the right of the western man.

We have always heard it as fanatical the fact that Muslims have the "obligation" to pray five times a day. On television we have seen enormous groups of men praying in the square. I was a long time in Libya before I managed to see someone praying and I even had to ask them to let me stay while they prayed and if they would allow me to photograph them. I also asked them to teach me to pray and the meaning of the prayers.

From the religious standpoint, Muslim prayer has a very deep mystical meaning and a great deal of symbolism. They stand to thank the Creator for the mountains that control the winds and rain. They bow down to thank Him for the animals, that they are meek. They touch the ground with their foreheads to thank Him for the

plants that bury their roots into the earth.

After having talked to many Muslims about this, I must say that my concept of the prayers changed radically.

It is clear that all the ancestral customs have a foundation and a purpose and the prayers of the Muslims are very healthy, in lay

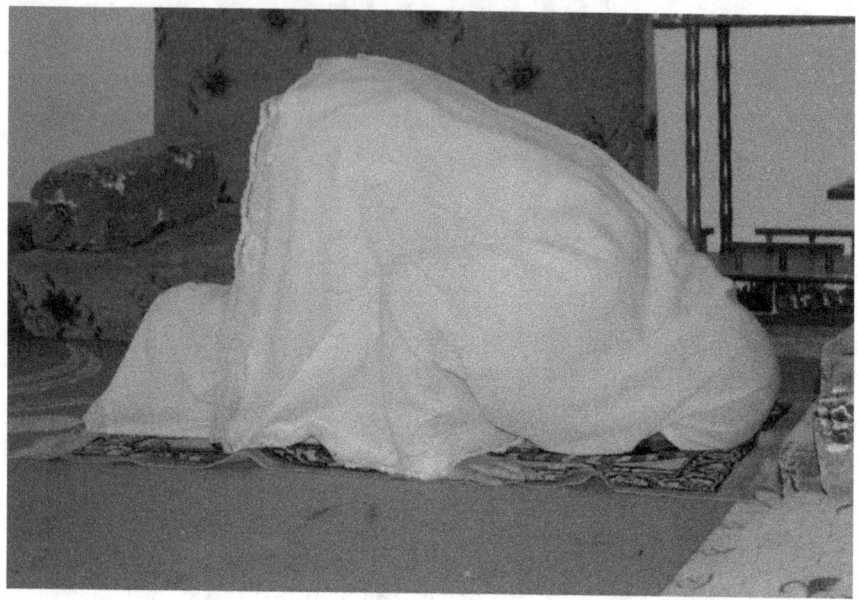

terms. Five times a day they do stretching exercises, they set themselves apart and free the mind of any problems.

In order to clear the mind, it is necessary to follow a ritual which, for them, consists in washing the hands and arms up to the elbow, the mouth, nose and ears, head and feet. Once this cleansing process has been followed, the women dress in clean clothes, different from what they are wearing.

Many Libyans have a sort of tunic that covers them from head to foot that is easy to put on and take off.

The put themselves on the small clean prayer mat, facing Mecca and say a prayer accompanied by stretching exercises. My words and explanations are tailored to the "non Muslim" so that they understand them but it is the reality seen from the outside.

Normally, in Libya they pray discreetly and it is not easy to see someone praying, except on Fridays in the Mosques. They even have a special designated room in the airports where those who wish to pray can go. I want to clarify this in view of the exhibitionism in which the west tries to make us believe.

Osama made two comparisons that seem very useful to me:

To interrupt daily life several times a day is healthy. For example, if you are discussing or negotiating with someone, suddenly you break off, you stop thinking about it for several minutes and when you return, the mind is clearer and you have lost that annoyance or pressure that prevented you from thinking freely.

He also made a very special remark that, when they withdraw to pray somewhere alone, even if it is only for a maximum of five minutes, they withdraw completely from the world and are used to that. They feel as if they are in God's hands, safe and protected. In other words, they know how to create this isolation and sensation of happiness that is so healthy.

On the other hand, it is necessary to point out that, in spite of the fact everyone says it is better to pray five times a day if possible, it is also certain, and I can prove this, that many times they will make two or three prayers into one because they have a job or are in a place where it is difficult to pray or wash themselves.

I have to say, with all of this I have never observed the fanaticism talked about so much and, quite to the contrary, I have observed exercises for spiritual withdrawal that are very healthy for the mind and body.

Belly Dancing

The understanding and approach to Arab culture, so near in terms of distance and yet so far in terms of information, is limited and very biased. We know everything that is happening and what they eat on the other side of the Atlantic, yet we know almost nothing about a country that is so near to ours in the same Mediterranean sea and less than 2 hours away by plane.

Most people do not even know where this country that is so hospitable, safe and magical is, and obviously they have a totally distorted view of it.

Belly dancing has always been one of those things shrouded in mystery with strange explanations relating to parties, important sheiks, harems and things of that nature.

On one occasion we were in the family home all seated on the floor in the main room enjoying a pleasant afternoon, happy and contented talking and playing with the children. Suddenly, they got up and asked me to go with them to one of the flexible rooms where they got out a large flat drum of the type that several people play at the same time while seated.

One of the sisters began to beat the drum quickly and very rhythmically. You could tell she had had a lot of practice. Another one of the girls grabbed one of those scarves that they wear on their heads, tied it around her thighs and began to move with fantastic grace and agility. She danced for a while until another sister got up and gestured to give her the scarf. She then began to dance. And so it went on, each one passing the scarf to the next and dancing for quite a while.

Everyone had their own style and all possessed astounding agility and flexibility. Wonderful!

Why were they dancing? Simply to have fun and, I would add, it is good exercise for the belly, waist, stomach, rhythm and so on. Seeing it for myself, I found that there were many movements that were much more attractive and sensual than those of the dancers who are on stage in the clubs.

I tried to follow the movements, however, I discovered they were not as easy as they looked at first glance. They are very different movements to what we are used to. Slowly but surely I began to learn and I loved it. What I have seen is that all the Libyan women that I have met know how to dance like that and they do it very well. They also dance at weddings and at their own private parties.

The Distorted Image

With each new experience in Libya I always ended up thinking about the difference between the image we westerners have of Libya and Muslims and the reality.

Once my younger sister came to the desert with some friends to enjoy a few days in the Sahara. They had to take a minibus from Tripoli to Sabha because there was a problem with the Alitalia plane and they arrived so late that they missed the plane from Tripoli to Sabha. One of the friends was so frightened that he kept looking at the Libyans as if they were all criminals and constantly made negative comments.

Nobody in Libya had done anything to him. Everyone had been friendly and welcoming while Alitalia (a western company) had messed them about cancelling their flight without any notice.

On arriving in Tripoli we all moved fast so that they could get to Sabha as soon as possible since they had already missed the plane due to Alitalia's fault.

We found a minibus that would take them straight to Sabha from Tripoli airport.

The journey between Tripoli and Sabha was done at night and most ended up sleeping as did this man. However, he was so frightened that he suddenly had a nightmare that they were being attacked and began to shout. He woke all the others up with a fright who also began to shout and everything happened so suddenly that even the Libyan driver swerved with the minibus. It was a dangerous situation where something bad could have happened, and all because of an absurd fear with no foundation.

The reality was that it was in the west where they had the problems because of the delays of the Italian airline, Alitalia. On the return they lost their luggage between Italy and Spain, whilst in Libya everything was fun with good treatment and hospitality.

Bread

Bread is the most important food in Libya because it is used for eating and also cutlery. The above photographs show authentic Libyan bread which is delicious, however, each day most Libyans buy loaves in large quantities for a very low price that are made by the government.

All the food shops have a counter near the entrance where they keep these loaves and the people come to buy them every day.

At first I went to buy bread at the shop near the house. I asked for two loaves because it already seemed a lot and the shopkeeper replied that I could not have them. I was surprised and thought that perhaps there was some problem because I was a foreigner, although I have to acknowledge that he had been perfectly friendly.

Again there was a misunderstanding because the shopkeeper could not imagine what my problem was. After several attempts on my part to buy the loaves, they explained to me that the minimum I could buy was 6 - 10 loaves and that they cost something like 0.3 LYD. (I can't remember the exact price anymore). I decided to leave and talk to my friends because it all seemed very strange to me and I took it as an excuse not to sell to me.

How could they tell me that I could only buy a minimum of 6 - 10 loaves of bread? What was I going to do with so much bread? My western interpretation was that this man was making an excuse not to sell me the bread. It never entered my mind that it was

94

normal to buy all that bread because I would only buy in those quantities if I was having a party at home with a lot of guests. They explained to me that the government cultivated the wheat in huge irrigated stretches of the desert, then they made these loaves of bread and sold them at nominal prices. They also explained that if an immigrant could not afford to buy the bread, they would give it to him. The Libyans use the bread not just for food but also to pick up food, just as we would in the west with a piece of cutlery.

My Libyan family would buy a sack of warm freshly baked loaves every morning. Usually there were some left over as they bought extra as a precaution in case many guests arrived.

The leftover bread from the table and any loaves from the day before were cut up and taken to the animals on the farm.

Libyans love these loaves which are similar to western baguettes but with hard crusts. I much prefer the Libyan or Egyptian bread which I find delicious.

My family bought the Libyan bread only for special festivities to allow it to harden and make one of the most important wedding

dishes: Ftad.

They prepare the stew and add the bread just before serving. Ftad stew is normally made with camel meat for weddings.

It is funny but each meal that I have tasted in Libya has an equivalent in Spanish cuisine. Where Ftad is concerned, we have the similar "sopas mallorquinas" or Mallorcan soup because we also use stale bread. The difference is that the Mallorcan stale bread bears no resemblance to the Libyan stale bread nor do we eat camel.

Normally Libyans cook on gas hobs like we do but when they celebrate a wedding or the end of mourning or Ead or any feast which many people will attend, they have huge cauldrons for cooking on the ground. And, as I mentioned, every meal has its Spanish version and one day I will do this: Get together Libyan and Mallorcan cooks and explore the differences and similarities in our dishes.

The outside of the houses is used a great deal because it is hardly ever cold in the south - perhaps two months of the year - and it is never a bitter cold so as to be unbearable. Furthermore, they are surrounded by high walls which allows for intimacy and it is like a private area, just as in the classic old Mallorcan homes. Perhaps this is an Arab influence and I have always liked it very much. Furthermore, if we compare our food to other Arab countries, it is different. For example, I found that the cous cous which we have always eaten in Spain was only the Moroccan cous cous while the Libyan cous cous is very different both in terms of the way it is made as well as its ingredients.

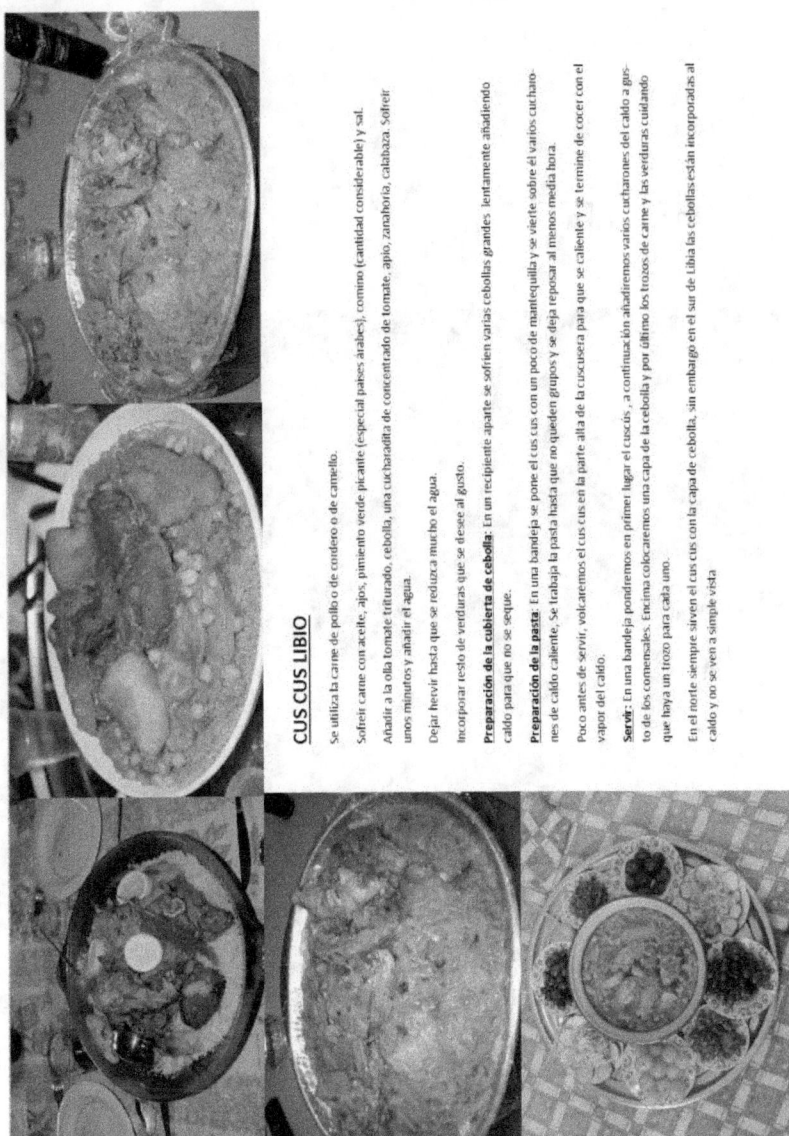

CUS CUS LIBIO

Se utiliza la carne de pollo o de cordero o de camello.

Sofreír carne con aceite, ajos, pimiento verde picante (especial países árabes), comino (cantidad considerable) y sal.

Añadir a la olla tomate triturado, cebolla, una cucharadita de concentrado de tomate, apio, zanahoria, calabaza. Sofreír unos minutos y añadir el agua.

Dejar hervir hasta que se reduzca mucho el agua.

Incorporar resto de verduras que se desee al gusto.

Preparación de la cubierta de cebolla: En un recipiente aparte se sofríen varias cebollas grandes lentamente añadiendo caldo para que no se seque.

Preparación de la pasta: En una bandeja se pone el cus cus con un poco de mantequilla y se vierte sobre él varios cucharones de caldo caliente. Se trabaja la pasta hasta que no queden grupos y se deja reposar al menos media hora.

Poco antes de servir, volcaremos el cus cus en la parte alta de la cuscusera para que se caliente y se termine de cocer con el vapor del caldo.

Servir: En una bandeja pondremos en primer lugar el cuscús , a continuación añadiremos varios cucharones del caldo a gusto de los comensales. Encima colocaremos una capa de la cebolla y por último los trozos de carne y las verduras cuidando que haya un trozo para cada uno.

En el norte siempre sirven el cus cus con la capa de cebolla, sin embargo en el sur de Libia las cebollas están incorporadas al caldo y no se ven a simple vista.

97

Ramadan

The reason for showing a photograph of the food served for breakfast during Ramadan is only because it is the first thought that comes to a westerner, that the Muslims hold large feasts during Ramadan, that they have huge orgies. On the other hand, I have heard that it is a fanatical custom, that they suffer so much and everyone uses the example of the poor Muslim mason who goes to work and almost faints without being able to eat or even drink water for the entire day.

First and foremost, I think it is important to make the distinction that it is not the same to observe the month of Ramadan in a country where people are predominantly Muslim, like in Libya, as it is for a Muslim in a western country where everything is more problematic.

The truth is that the Libyans that I know celebrate the month of Ramadan with joy and look forward to its arrival, even the children. It is a very special month much like joining the Christmas and August summer holidays together.

The first thing everyone does is to request their holidays during the month of Ramadan and some companies slow down their business as we do here in the summer when, for example, the courts and schools close and more and more companies choose to close during this time.

Since the majority of the population is Muslim, the country adapts to the fasting in Ramadan as it is an important part of the month.

We know that they fast from dawn until sundown and this is usually from five o'clock in the morning until about seven o'clock in the evening, depending on the date that Ramadan falls.

This sounds horrible, having to fast for so many hours in the heat of the Saharan summer without so much as a drink of water , however, things are not exactly like that when you have grown up accustomed to this fast.

Most activity during the month of Ramadan begins after breaking the Ramadan fast which is usually around eight o'clock in the evening and everything stays open until four in the morning. It is at night when people go shopping, to the doctor or to visit relatives or to do those things that for the rest of the year they do during the day. Of course, since they go to bed so late, they get up as late as possible and start their normal day slowly in a relaxed way preparing the Ramadan breakfast, taking care of the children, house etc. but calmly until the time to break their fast.

After spending the day without eating, they cannot fill themselves with food as that would cause stomach pains, so they usually start with a date and some milk, next they say the prayers for that time of day and then go back to starting their breakfast little by little. More or less every two hours throughout the night, they keep on eating until they go to bed around three or four o'clock in the morning.

If we stop and think, it is not much to reverse our waking hours. Normally, it is more difficult during the first few days and then afterwards it becomes totally natural. Sometimes at the beginning, people complain of headaches or thirst. However, they know very well that they must not damage their health. If a woman is pregnant or menstruating, if someone is old or ill or travelling or simply feels they cannot go on, then they do not need to fast. There are so many options that really those who fast are the ones who do it with pleasure and because they want to.

It is fun to watch the children who all want to emulate the grown ups but logically they do not have the willpower or maturity to do so. I remember a boy of 12 who each day told me he was going to fast and at midday I would see him with a huge sandwich, while nobody said one word to him. These things are between a person and Allah (God) and nobody judges if you can or cannot keep the fast.

Ramadan is also a month for meetings, forgiveness and reflection and this also happened in my family. The relatives that lived far away would appear one after another at the time for breaking the fast so we had to be prepared with lots of food each day.

I remember there were two sisters who had not spoken to one another for a long time and when the month of Ramadan arrived, suddenly I saw how they hugged and began to speak again.

The families also give to someone poor whom they know, according to their own financial situation without it representing a sacrifice. My family would take a lamb from their farm that they had slaughtered and cut into pieces to a widow who had many children and to whom any help would be welcome.

Conversations revolved around the future and in turn on the mistakes made in life, above all I experienced this with Osama and Mannar who were closest to me and who would explain all these intimate things. They did not explicitly tell me that they were making an "examination of their conscience" but I know about the past, their mistakes and illusions primarily from Ramadans in subsequent years that I have experienced in Libya.

The Muslims do not go to confession to relieve their consciences like practising Catholics. Instead they go direct to God hoping and trusting that Allah in all his mercy will give them forgiveness. The month of Ramadan is precisely the month of the year in which each person will look at himself before God and make promises to improve on those things in which he believes he has done wrong.

It is also the month to get together with friends or relatives with whom there have been problems. Surprisingly, and in the areas of Libya where I have lived, I have found that all the people I have met observe this month in the same way.

The end of Ramadan is very important. All Libyans who can, will get together in the city of their Tribe. They will buy new clothes which they will wear on that day and all the children will receive presents.

If we now add all of this together and take into account that they are immersed in a tribal society, perhaps we can then understand the different perspective from which they view and cope with this month that is so special to Islam.

One of the things that I enjoyed most during Ramadan was to go out window shopping around 10 o'clock at night because the entire city was lit up, the streets full of people, all of the shops open and with a lot of new merchandise because they know that families, even with little money, will go out shopping. You experience a festive atmosphere at a time when normally you would be asleep or at least relaxing at home.

I think that the reversal of schedule each year for Ramadan is the reason why time is not so important in Libya because you gradually get into a new schedule little by little beginning before Ramadan and afterwards gradually getting back to the daytime schedule. At the same time, this makes the body and mind more flexible with regard to the time for eating and sleeping and not like us who have a time schedule that is fairly constant throughout our lives.

A foreigner who comes to Libya during the month of Ramadan and goes out shopping during the day will get a huge surprise:

On the other hand, if they knew they could take advantage of all the open shops during the night, they would understand things a little better. In Libya it is very easy because there is no law but instead the lives of the majority of Libyans who have been adapting to their needs and it is very important to remember that, at the end of the day, you can do the same things as in any month of the year, except at a different time.

It would always come as a surprise when at 10 o'clock at night someone would say, "I'm off to the dentist".

From my point of view, these time changes for all Libyans, including children in spite of the fact they do not fast but go to bed at the same time as the adults, make people more flexible as regards timetables and sometimes, I think, a little unruly.

Fasting during Ramadan is not seen as a punishment neither as a great sacrifice because it is something they have seen in the family and country since birth and they know how to observe it in a sensible way.

The first time I went to Libya during Ramadan, they asked me what I wanted to do. I felt courageous and willing to fast along with them, however, they made it clear that it was not necessary because I was not a Muslim and nobody would look down on me if I ate something. I told them, however, that I wanted to experience everything with them and that I would do it. Nobody said anything and Mannar advised me to get up at 4 o'clock in the morning, eat a hearty breakfast and then go back to bed and get up as late as I could.

I went to bed ready to follow this advice and fast with them but it is not necessary to clarify that my sleeping habits are different to theirs. I was used to getting up and going to bed early. The night before Ramadan, however, we had stayed up very late so I was not able to get up at 4 o'clock for breakfast. Afterwards, around 8 o'clock I had eyes like saucers and could not sleep again.

Just thinking that I could not eat or drink for the whole day made me hungry and thirsty and I was not tired enough to go back to sleep. I went out to find the streets deserted and very hot. I went back home and everyone was still asleep, so I decided to sit down and write a little but the whole time in the back of my mind was the fact that I had not had breakfast and would not eat again until evening.

Suddenly, around 11 o'clock my friend, Mannar, appeared in my "flexible room" with a huge tray of milk, coffee, green tea, fresh mango juice, hot bread, home made butter, two fried eggs, French fries, biscuits and, I suppose, other things but I cannot remember. What is certain is that my hand went straight to the tray and without feeling embarrassed or guilty I sat on the ground and had the best breakfast in my life. The pleasure was immeasurable. I ate slowly and enjoyed every mouthful.

Libyan food is delicious because, in general, they use fresh produce like the mango juice which is made the moment they pick the fruit from the enormous trees in garden. These mangoes are sweet and smell wonderful. I love to peel them using my teeth because when you take the first bite they impart a wonderfully intense smell and taste. The butter is home made, the eggs come from their chickens at the farm I have already mentioned that eat left over bread and grass. They have no idea what chicken feed is.

The children love the mangoes and not all of the houses have mango trees in their gardens, so it was normal to hear the doorbell and, on opening, find a group of children from the neighbourhood who had come to ask for a mango. Every time I was there, they would give mangoes to all the children who wanted them. They were not begging but just neighbours who dreamed of a sweet mango instead of doughnuts.

Telephones in Libya

There once was a man attached to a phone…

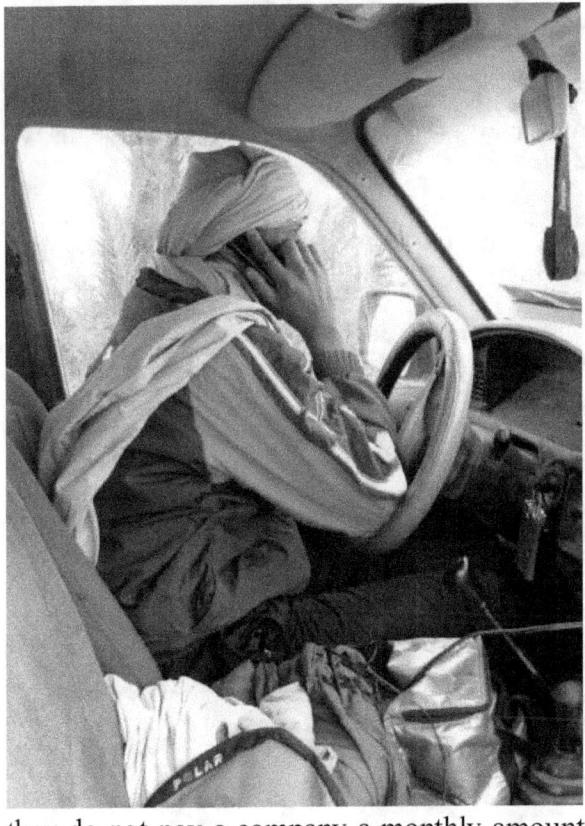

I have never met people more addicted to the telephone than the Libyans. Perhaps because it was their first technological toy after living in a society that had not yet fallen into the vortex of consumer spending. It is surprising how many functions they can get out of the telephone and things that they do that I would never even remotely have thought of.

To start with, they do not pay a company a monthly amount for their mobiles but instead buy cards worth 5 or 10 LYD which they introduce using the code on the card. They also transfer money from one telephone to another using a series of numbers.

On the other hand, the landline is free. The government gave them to the families so that they could speak to other members of their tribe, that is to say, their extended family since being in a country where everyone is so spread out, communication is difficult.

Every Libyan has a mobile phone which they always carry in their hand with various cards which they keep on changing. They use the mobile phone cards to store their photographs or simply because they have several numbers.

They use the mobile's camera a great deal, the hands free microphone feature so as not to have to hold it or so that other members of the family can listen as well. I have also seen babies chewing on them or dribbling on their mother's phone so that afterwards they did not work and had to be opened and dried out.

The telephone is a work tool for all Libyans more important than agencies or newspapers as the most important means of information.

They hear of everything by phone across the tribal network and, when I say everything, I really mean everything that goes on

from government to street level. Everything runs over the tribal and telephone networks. Precisely for this reason NATO bombed the communication antennas and succeeded in cutting off the Libyans.

The telephone is the main tool for work and entertainment.

During a visit to some friends, they gave me a photo taken on the telephone because I forgot to mention that Libyans always give you presents when you visit them:

Their telephones have many uses although they are always different to ours because their tastes are different.

So, if the shops are open, during the day or night, people will spend time shopping. In my particular case, I wanted to have a little food set aside in case I was hungry and wanted a snack or to give something sweet to a child but for some mysterious reason, I never managed it. I would go to the supermarket and buy something and when I got home I met lots of people who were willing to try what I had bought, most especially if I had bought ice cream or sweets for the children, so that in the end there was nothing left for me.

This happened a lot with watermelons. As I have already mentioned, the watermelons in the south of Libya are cultivated on irrigated government land. They are the best watermelons I have ever tasted. I would leave the greengrocer's whose owner was an Egyptian, and which was only about 100 metres from my house. I would buy a huge watermelon and in the blink of an eye, there was no watermelon anymore. I did that many times and the same thing always happened. One day I even bought several huge watermelons thinking that it would be impossible to finish them all… and so it was. They did not finish them but when I went to eat the rest of them a few hours later, they were all gone.

Jealousy in Tribal Societies

Despite having extolled the virtues of the Libyan tribal society, I have to recognize that they are people and therefore have their weaknesses. One of the problems that I was able to observe was jealousy between people in the same community and how the rules of cohabitation make aggressive behavior more difficult. They have, however, created means of obtaining results, depending on the type of situation, without direct confrontation.

In a family home, each person has their own role and they know it very well. I noticed this immediately when I arrived at the house and it prevented me from daring to do certain things.

I really wanted to prepare a Spanish meal for them but despite commenting on it several times, I did not perceive any interest on their part. They told me that I could do whatever I wanted however, things were so well organized that I did not see how I could become a part of it all without upsetting or pushing someone out.

I mentioned this to my guide in these things, that is to say, Osama, and, as he does not get involved in the running of the family home, he told me not to worry about it at all and that I should simply go to the corner shop, buy the ingredients that were not in the house, and make a sweet cake which they really like and, that way, everyone would be delighted and appreciative.

However, things were not as easy as Osama had told me because I followed the first steps, telling the family that I was going to make a cake and asking where some of the ingredients were which I know they already had. Suddenly, and I don't know when this happened but two sisters began making cakes for the family so there was not enough room in the kitchen. I therefore stopped for a while until they had finished. I then continued with my carrot cake and when it was ready for baking, I asked which oven to put it in. After an hour, I thought it strange that I could not smell the cake. I went to the oven and to my enormous surprise the oven temperature was on 30 C, so I raised the temperature and asked what had happened. Nobody knew a thing. I checked again after half an hour and the oven was again almost at room temperature. I don't know how many times I kept raising the temperature until I finally said why was someone lowering the temperature. Nobody knew what I was talking about. I intimated what I felt to my closest friends but they said that surely it was some sort of mistake.

After 6 hours, I took the carrot cake out of the oven and even now Osama laughs about my cake and made the whole family laugh, of course kindly. I have made this cake so many times at home and it had never failed. Furthermore, the baking time is approximately one and a half hours, never 6 - and even then it was undercooked. We could think that the oven was broken, however, the strange thing is that the cakes of the two other women were perfectly baked and the next day the oven was working again.

What happened? Who was jealous of the possible success of my cake?

My thinking is that the fact I was a foreigner and coming to a home with many new things made me the centre of attention something that jealous people cannot abide. For better or worse, when they saw their special role in the kitchen under threat, they decided "to fight" so as not to allow it to be "snatched away".

Many years later I asked again what they thought had happened, although I know what happened without knowing who did it. However, whether out of discretion or out of the desire not to create problems, nobody told me a thing and I did not press them.

I have observed many situations like this which involve theoretical confrontations between people but things always end up with no raised voices or aggressive behavior.

On another occasion several sisters and I were going to visit Osama's girlfriend. Sara mentioned that she wanted to come. Osama took one look at what she was wearing and told her to please go and change because what she was wearing was awful. This was a verbal exchange between siblings and therefore of no real importance but she was dressed quite extravagantly and Osama did not want her visiting his girlfriend dressed like that. Sara was not willing to change her clothes and very politely told him so. Osama, however, insisted that he did not like what she was wearing. So, Sara, in a soft voice and with no sign of annoyance or anger, simply bent her head to one side and said that she had a headache, did not feel well and therefore would not be going to visit Osama's girlfriend.

The others said nothing, there was no comment and I was surprised how they could have believed that Sara suddenly had a headache. After a few hours, I could not resist asking Osama if he really believed that Sara had had a headache to which he answered that he did not know but that is what she had said. I explained my point of view and he said that it could be true and then changed the subject.

In few words they were telling me that it was not my concern and that during the clash both knew what was going on but neither of the two wanted to give way. There was no need to say anything directly, nor insult or offend. Both had made their positions clear and then carried on being friends as if nothing had happened.

When a man marries, his wife and descendents will become a part of his tribe.

Said like this, it sounds a little sad that they are separating from the woman's family. In reality, however, nothing changes. It is true that there are rules that everyone knows but the woman feels very comfortable with her own sisters and relatives so she goes and visits them very often and spends several days with them, especially if there is an imminent birth or wedding or to cleanse herself during menstruation. The newlyweds also spend several days in the family home of the husband and there, too, jealousies can arise.

According to what I have observed, the same thing has happened to all the new women who have come into my house. On arrival they make a special effort to be another daughter or they try to help with the everyday chores of the house and in no time I hear negative comments about them. This happens too in our society where family conflicts between cousins or mothers-in-laws almost make up part of a tradition.

I understand that these women bring new customs to the home but I also think there are feelings of jealousy from both sides. If there is a small clash, then it is a disaster because the whole family gets involved and meets hundreds of times until the situation is resolved but in the process every problem comes out.

I would say that in many Libyan families there is no need for psychologists because if a healing word is what we psychologists think is necessary, then in Libya everyone heals each other. I am reminded of something that happened to me that no psychologist or psychiatrist could have done better.

During my stay in the house I had started to make close ties with most of the sisters and the parents, however, a few days before I was due to return to Spain, I realized that I had been there over a month and yet had not made much progress with my study project and the goals I had set for myself before leaving. I also must have felt sad because I had to leave and yet still had so much to do. My face must also have changed and I spent a lot of time in my room with my paperwork and computer until, after a few days, Osama appeared at the family home and came to see me looking very serious. He told me that he needed to speak to me so we sat down and then he asked me what was going on with me, what had his sisters done to me? His tone and questions surprised me a great deal so my replies were questions more to be able to understand what he meant. He explained that the whole family had been calling him constantly and everyone was sad because I was not talking to them, that I was punishing them and they did not know what they had done. Even Toraya had I said that the foot massage I had given her was with much less feeling. Osama asked me to tell him what had happened. Once I had recovered from my surprise at his and the family's words, I told him that I was really sorry and that nobody had done anything at all to upset me. I then went on to explain what I was feeling and why I was sad.

Then Osama got cross with me and said that I had learned absolutely nothing about Libyans or Libya after all the time I had spent in that house. How could this be? He explained to me that whenever someone has a problem, whoever it was, they ask for help and those who are around help them. I was telling him that I had a problem, however, I had not asked anyone for help with my feelings of sadness therefore the whole family could only suppose that I was upset with them.

On understanding the situation I had created, I left the room, called together the whole family and asked them to forgive me and explained to them what was going on. I cried, they cried, we all cried then we hugged and carried on crying! It was wonderful therapy! When we stopped crying and hugging, I felt like new and the sadness had left me. I felt understood and supported as I have never felt before.

From then on, I know that I always have to explain to those around me if I have a problem and, many times they will call me on the telephone or when I am there, they will call me to tell me their problems because they need to get them off their chests.

I know that everyone confides things at certain moments but in Libya it is more than that. Possibly due to the great empathy shown when conversing with each other, it is a habit acquired through living together that is carried out on a daily basis.

Many family problems are due to the great changes that have come about in the last generations.

Let us imagine a woman like Khadija, married at 15 and having one child after another until she has 15. A woman who never went to school, who as a child lived in an adobe house and ate dates and Basin. (Buns made with flour, water and a little fat).

Nearly all this woman's children are university graduates, have several kilos of gold jewelry, a big house in Wadi Shati, her tribal city, another in Sabha where they usually live and a farm some 8 kms from Sabha where Osama lives.

There is a 180 degree difference in what she currently enjoys to the environment in which she grew up. Khadija is a woman with a positive attitude towards life. Calm and hardworking, she is tireless. She loves to go to the farm every evening to visit her son, Osama, take leftover food to the animals, look after the chickens and work a little in the vegetable garden.

Khadija has never read a book or a newspaper. One day she told me that she felt uncomfortable when she saw her children studying when they were small and yet was never able to help them. She was very happy that all her children could study and, in turn help their own children, and have more opportunities.

Her open mind is very healthy and thanks to the changes that took place in Libya, all her children were able to study, travel and create their own futures. However, this change did not come without a price.

The intellect of the children is not the same as that of the parents no matter how much respect and love they feel for them. This is possibly the biggest problem with the new Libyan generation. On the one hand, they respect their elders, love them dearly and remain close to them but, on the other hand, they have all their needs taken care of and they have different knowledge, new ways of life, new technologies and capabilities. All of these many times leave them confused and not knowing what to do. A new perspective has been born, new boundaries that have brought about a certain bewilderment. This is the field which was beginning to interest me more and more as I stayed there, to the extent that I spent more time talking about it and observing the generational differences and consequences of the harsh changes taking place, than in the development of a child's personality in a tribal setting.

Nearly all the young people have gone to university and many afterwards even went abroad to study a post graduate degree.

Something quite singular and special has occurred in a country that has been closed to the west as "punishment" from the United States, keeping it isolated for years. This is due to the fact that its young people have grown up in universities - quite often foreign - and have brought back new customs to add to the old ones that are still very much alive because just 40 years before they were all that they had.

Obviously nobody is perfect and all situations can be improved, but I start from the premise that we are not judges who can spend time saying what mistakes and things can be improved in every culture because, furthermore, you have to understand that each change causes a chain reaction of unforeseeable changes and this is precisely what is happening in Libya.

A culture and a people prospering and developing, maintaining its traditions and social customs without fully becoming a consumer society, produces many positive results that, if properly understood, would make it impossible to believe that a people with these characteristics could be fanatical or aggressive or that they would allow themselves to be manipulated, as those from the outside are wanting us to believe.

I know of no-one who has been in Libya who can imagine, not by a long shot, what it is really like because inevitably, when we look at others, we always interpret what we see from our own experiences or frame of reference. The Libyan frames of reference, history, culture and experiences are a long way from ours and a cultural spokesperson would be necessary to properly come to agreement on initiating a dialogue.

When I read information on Libya in the West I always ask myself whether the person writing does not know the country or has

Casas de adobe de la Libya de hace más de 40 años.
Wadi Ash Shati

Pueblo actual de la libia de la jamahiriyah.
Wadi Ash Shati

Ejemplo de casa en Wadi Ash Shati

Miles de casas y edificios con las últimas tecnologías incorporadas, listas para ser inauguradas en 2011

been to the country without really knowing anyone, or is really trying to give a biased version of what it is really like in Libya. I suppose that it is a little bit of all this.

Only starting from the development of Libyan houses in the south, as an example, can we see the great changes that have come about. In the small towns and cities of the south it is surprising to see alongside the old medinas where people lived 40 years before, the present towns and a little further away on the outskirts the thousands of houses that have been built with the very best materials and latest technology for handing over to Libyans at the end of 2011. It was surprising to go visit these houses under construction because, as I have already said, they had reverse osmosis systems to purify the water.

It is clear evidence of the importance of the home to Libyans, which is a right, and all families are owners of at least one house and, furthermore, many more own a farm (oasis) where they cultivate the land and keep animals.

My family had a farm (oasis) about 8 km from the house together with many other families because the government had given many farms years ago to the Libyans who had asked for them, but any Libyan could fence off an area of the desert for cultivation, drilling one or two wells and start farming. He would then recognize this land as his and receive deeds to the property.

Many of the families that I know have a farm where they grow watermelons, melons, courgettes, beetroot, oranges, lemons, mandarin oranges, mangoes and grapes. Usually there were many palms in these farms which are highly prized by the Libyans, as well as land for planting fodder for the animals.

In addition, they keep sheep, goats, chickens, donkeys and some dogs. It is funny but all the dogs I have seen in Libya look the same and the majority are wild. Dogs are considered dirty in Libya and never allowed in the house. However, in the country they are used to look after the sheep and keep an eye on the farm.

I am not surprised that they do not allow animals to come into the home, as we do in the west, because they sit on the floor. Many times I have thought about sitting on the floor to eat like in Libya but I never do precisely because of my dog who lives in the house.

In my home we have always had dogs but I have to recognize that it would be impossible to sit or eat seated on the floor like the Libyans do, not only because it would be difficult to control where the dog went but also because of our own customs.

Property and Farms

Many times I have heard it said that in Libya you have no right to own property because it is a communist country. This is a comment from someone who does not know Libya.

What is true is that a political party is a totally artificial organization created by politicians or aspiring politicians in order to manipulate or set themselves apart from others.

In Libya, on the other hand, how the country functions stems naturally as a response to the life and resources of the country and is developed by the Libyans themselves, the government and the tribes through their leaders.

While we have to hand over part of our profits working to maintain our institutions, our politicians, build roads, infrastructure, etc., in Libya everything is paid for from the oil which is considered a national asset belonging to all Libyans.

As a result, in my opinion, the people's struggle is greater for us than them and for the little effort that their government and tribal leaders make, the people have immense benefits and a much easier life.

Some will reply that they are lucky because they have oil. However, not in all countries with oil reserves are these resources socialized and benefiting all levels of the population. Of course, I am talking of the Libya that I knew before the U.S. and NATO invaded the country, a country in which the education of its young people in colleges and universities was its priority and for this reason education was free at all levels.

Food was available in a large network of state shops and was subsidized with symbolic prices. Then if they wanted to by other food items which were not necessities, they could purchase them in private shops. Having a home was a constitutional right. Every Libyan had the right to a house and this was a reality. Furthermore, the houses were large in keeping with their way of life. Healthcare was free as was water and electricity. However, to Libyans this was just a form of distributing the benefits of a common asset belonging to them all: oil.

About 5 years ago, I experienced a situation in which an important part of the Libyan tribes and a part of the government in which the Libyan leader, Moammar al Gadafi, wanted to change the way of sharing out the benefits of the oil to the Libyans. Many Libyans felt that too much money would be lost "along the way". For more than a year I heard the Libyans giving their opinions on this, even teenagers.

There were a lot meetings and discussions between the government and tribes because the group that wanted the change wanted the profits from the petrol handed over directly to all Libyans and then each Libyan would be responsible for his share and would pay college, hospital and all his expenses out of it. The idea was that every Libyan would manage his share and thus avoid the corruption that had been detected. The reality is that they could not make the change because an important part of the government and the tribes would not accept it.

From my standpoint and what I experienced, I believe it was a much more democratic decision than what we are used to in Spain.

Marriage and Monogamy

When talking about Arabs, in the west some topics have become so generalized it is as if Arabs were all the same and all the Arab countries cut from the same cloth and creating clones.

One of the things that surprises the most is the generalized idea of polygamy in Islamic societies.

After spending years in Libya, I never managed to meet any man who had several wives, nor did I hear comments about politicians or wealthy individuals with several wives. I never heard anyone talk about a "harem" - a word with which we are so familiar in the west.

When I felt more confident, I one day asked a mother of 15 children in my Libyan family how she would feel if her husband took a second wife. Her face was a picture as she was so surprised by the question and, after smiling politely, she told me she would not like it at all.

I kept on asking and looking in books to find out where the western media had got this idea from that had become so widespread.

When the prophet Mahoma (Mohammed 570 - 632 AD) received the word of God, the country was going through a difficult situation in which there were constant tribal wars and many deaths. The result was that many women with children were left alone without the resources to survive in an inhospitable area that is the Saudi Arabian desert. Mohama wanted to organize that problematic society so that the men who could, would take care of those widows.

He himself took various women under his protection, even elderly women, for example, when history tells us that he was very close to his wife, Hadijah, who supported him in all he did.

The Libyans explained that these laws in the Koran refer to very specific cases and must be governed by many rules and always with the consent of the wife.

If the husband pressures the wife to allow him to marry a second wife, she can divorce him and receive support from the government.

They explained several possibilities to me such as a terminally ill wife who could give her permission for her husband to marry a second wife with the understanding that she would care for the children and be with him, since the wife could not.

On the other hand, however, the Koran requires that the husband gives exactly the same to each wife. It is at this point that the Libyans with whom I have spoken smile and say, if it is difficult to have one wife, what would it be like to have more than one and then they say, "oooh, impossible, just too much trouble".

Another reason why I find this option an impossibility in Libya, for the people that I have met, is that the women manage the house and family money.

What is more, if we start from an emotional level, Libyan culture places great value and respect on childbearing, as I have already commented. The men, in addition to loving their wives, have a great respect for them as the mother of their children.

In short, what I want to point out is that I have never seen a Libyan with two wives and once I researched this option, I have discovered a hundred reasons why it is impossible in Libya. I have, however, known men and women who are divorced.

Divorce is approached in a very different way from us. When a man and a woman decide to divorce, they only have to say so and each one goes to his own home. Then the wife's tribe plays a role. They have meetings with the husband and wife in front of the relatives who act as arbiters, in which they talk for hours or days on the reasons the couple wish to separate, trying to understand the one who does not belong to the family.

Normally, after a few days or weeks, both will return to the home and try to resolve their problems after this "group therapy".

If the meeting with the wife's family is not enough, then the husband's family can become involved and continue with the meetings. If they separate three times, it is then considered that the marriage is finally over.

I have met many couples who have separated once or twice but after family meetings have not gone as far as divorcing.

I have asked many times what is discussed in these meetings and how they work and I have recognized that it is a true form of group therapy.

The Camel Trains

One of my dreams, as yet unfulfilled, has been to travel with one of the camel trains that cross the Sahara desert from the savannahs of Niger and Chad to Sabha.

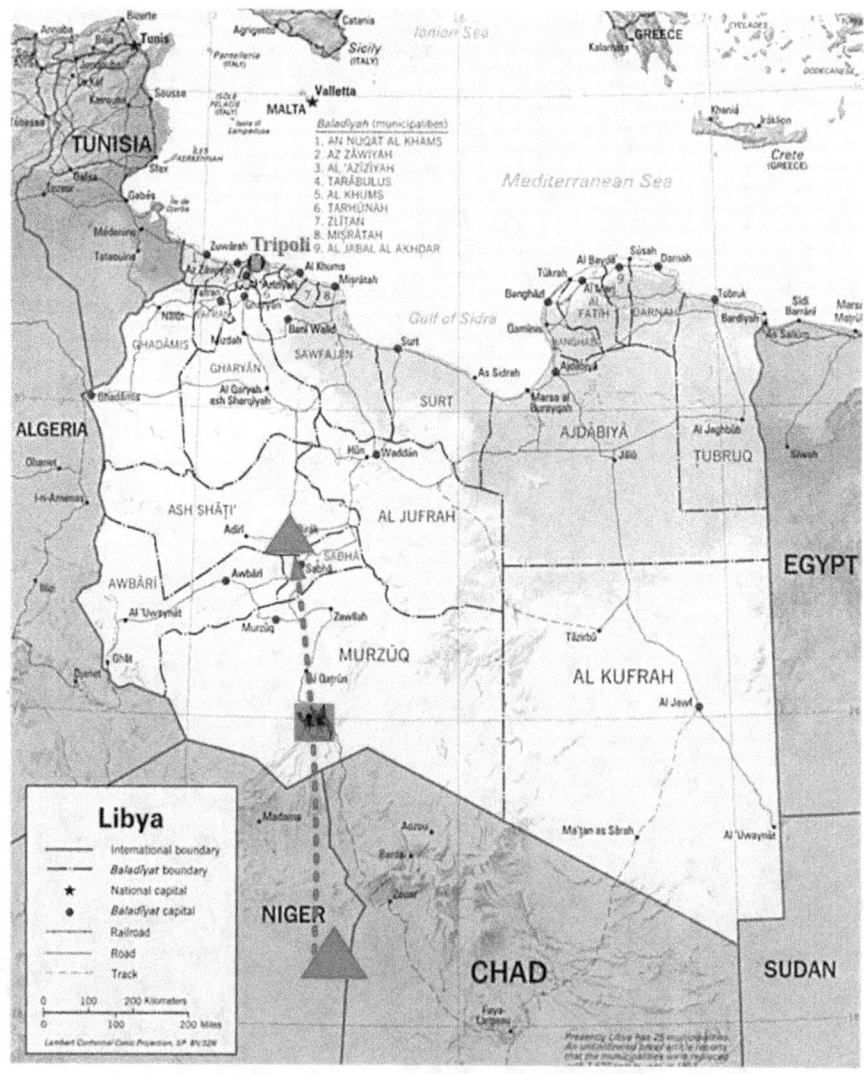

The Libyans use camels a great deal allowing them to graze

seemingly unattended in the desert because they have excellent memories and will always return to where they have been given food and water. I have never been in any place in the desert where there have not been signs of camels. At first I thought they were

wild camels because it seemed impossible that these camels,

hundreds of kilometers from any town, actually had an owner.
However, they do, and their owner knows each one of them and
always knows where they are, if they have a female about to give

birth, or even where they are all scattered about. There are even camel farms where you can buy their milk.

The thousands of kilometers of Libyan Sahara at first appear abandoned and inhospitable but, when you get to know certain areas, you realize that you can find wells, tanks, cisterns and reservoirs where the animals can go and drink and people can fill their water containers or bathe.

We would stop at these for a shower, to wash our clothes or to fill our water containers for the road. There were always animals nearby.

Two of these water reserves in front of the grand massif of Murzuq have a small house where a person lives paid for by the government. According to what I was told, they spend time there alone and then go home for their holidays.

I had a funny experience with one of these water reserve caretakers because at various times I had been there, on his invitation, and spent several hours sitting on the ground next to the fire drinking tea and talking about all sorts of things. One or two years later I returned to the same water hole and I realized that I must have changed a little, something which seemed normal to me after the time that had elapsed, but I began to have a strange feeling of confusion because the man who used to invite us for tea had changed a great deal but, at the same time, was still the same. I could not figure this out and it made no sense to me. At the end, when we said our goodbyes, I explained to Osama what I had been feeling during the visit to the water reserve... I was hugely surprised by his reply, "This is not the usual watering hole that we visit most of the time, but another one that is on the other side of the Massif de Murzuq and this caretaker is the brother of the one you know."

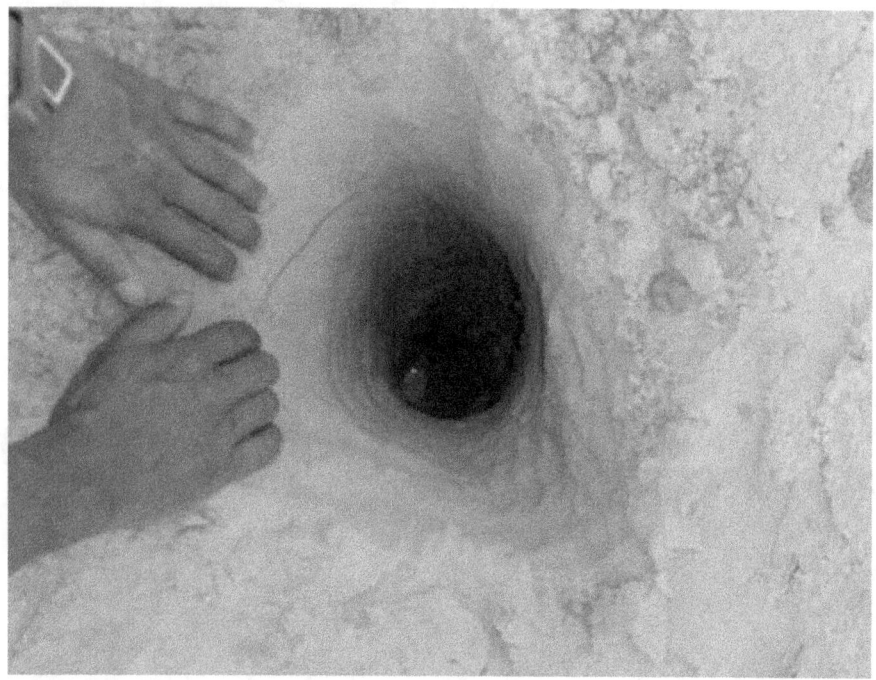

My greatest puzzlement had been that the two men had appeared the same yet I had always heard the first one stuttering slightly and, on my last visit, it seemed that this small problem had disappeared.

I have tried camel's milk twice. The first time I was surprised at how bitter and what a strong flavour it had, while the second time the taste seemed sweeter and more mild. I was told that this was normal because the flavour varied depending on what the camel had been eating or drinking.

Camel meat is prized by Libyans and for this reason a bridegroom will usually give one or two camels to the family of his future wife for the wedding festivities and he will also purchase several camels for his own family for the celebrations.

When they told me about where the camels had come from and I saw them arrive, I felt a great desire to follow their journey. I was told that it was somewhat difficult to do this as the journey is very hard and the people who bring them are very rough with their own ways that could, perhaps, make the trip difficult.

I understand that to join a community you must know it very well and adapt as much as possible to its ways. For this reason I began asking more and more about the trans Saharan crossings of the camel trains.

The camels from Chad and Niger graze, fatten up and become strong during the rainy season from June to October in the Nguigmi savannah in southeast Niger. This region borders with Chad. When the desert temperatures begin to cool off a little, the camels are then taken to the Nguigmi markets in Niger. Most people consider this the largest camel market in the world, so buyers come from as far away as Kuwait, Al Baharem, Saudi Arabia, Libya etc.

Libyans interested in buying camels will go there and they will choose the ones they like the best. For the most part, they will buy males and some females producing a lot of milk, at least 10 litres a day. Once the camels have been bought, you have to pay a guide/herdsman who will take them from Niger to Sabha, travelling for two months across the desert.

Every group of camels corresponds to one buyer, or several, if they join together to form one train and pay the same guide/herdsman. Sometimes a maximum of up to three guides can go simultaneously. They travel in front of the train, on occasions up to one day ahead. These guides ride on their own camels with their own clothes and food, directing the route of the entire train and deciding where they should rest or stop for the night.

Each buyer will hire a car or truck in which he will take feed for the camels along the way in areas that are accessible. Each group knows what food is theirs and this is always respected.

The journey across the desert takes exactly 60 days.

The experience is hard on the animals, despite the fact they will find food at certain points along the way. They leave Niger strong and fat and arrive in Sabha emaciated. For this reason, the train will stay for a few days on the outskirts of the town so the animals can recuperate, fatten up, rest a little and then go to the markets in Sabha in better condition.

The Nguigmi region is the ideal place for the breeding and rearing of camels and it is inhabited by Arabs who concentrate solely on this business.

Every Friday there is a market where you can buy camels. There you can find huge males for breeding who can weigh up to 1,000 kilos as they receive a lot of care and attention in order to obtain more money for their future sale. Each day these males are given camel milk, sometimes up to twenty litres a day, in addition to consuming the same grass and feed as the rest of the animals.

During the cold months the animals are left to roam and begin to pair up. The male will choose a female and will not leave her until she is pregnant. They are very jealous and can kill if anybody gets close to his female. Their teeth are larger than those of a lion, measuring up to 5 cms. There have even been cases where they have killed humans. Once the female is pregnant, they both lose interest in each other and the male will look around for another female.

In June, with the rains, the grass grows in the Savannah and the males lose all interest in the females and go off to eat wherever they can.

As we know, the digestive system of the camel is quite different to any other animal since it has three chambers to the stomach which allow it to digest various types of food and extract the maximum amount of moisture from plants in order to receive the necessary water for its metabolism.

Everything it consumes is stored in its humps in the form of fat which can weigh up to 40 kilos and from which it sustains itself in times when there is no food. A camel can consume up to 75 or 80 litres of water and as much food as possible and can therefore refill its humps.

The females who became pregnant the year before will give birth to their babies as the gestational period for a camel is one year. Up until October they will have an abundance of food for their offspring and to recover from the long pregnancy all during the rainy season when the savannah is covered in grass.

Some males are kept enclosed so that they cannot roam on the savannah and instead they keep them well fed for sale at the market. At this market you will find many different types of camels and they are always full of merchants who will buy them for resale in their own country or for personal business.

Usually the camels chosen to take across the Sahara to the large market in the Libyan city of Sabha are 4 or 5 years old and generally male because the Libyans consume a great deal of camel meat.

The above photograph is of a group of camels on the outskirts of Sabha who are being fed. Their owners, together with the guides, will check the animals, talk about any incidents that have taken place, whether there have been any losses and tell stories.

Everyone, camels as well as humans, recuperate from the journey.

These men are preparing the food for the camels who are about to arrive.

They say that during the long days of the journey the animals are so hungry that they will fight for the dregs of tea that the guides throw out. There are 20 days during the trip where the areas are so inaccessible that the trucks cannot get to them to leave them feed so the camels only eat the grass that they have been able to take on board and obviously it is very little compared to what an animal of this size is used to eating. This is the most difficult point of the journey. Sometimes they even try to eat the guides' clothing.

Each night when they stop to rest, they have to tie the hooves of the camels because if not, many of them would get up and wander off in search of food or return home.

With so many days walking without stopping, many things can happen like several camels losing the skin from their hooves, so the guides make protective socks which formerly were from camel skin but nowadays tend to be made from old truck tyres.

At times in the morning there are some camels that are so tired they cannot get up. If they are in a place that is accessible to the feed truck, then they will put the animal in the truck. Other times if the area is not able to be reached by truck, they will put a mark on the body of the camel as a sign of ownership, leave him with a pile of grass and will carry on the journey because they know that the animal will rest, eat and when he has recuperated will follow them or return back to where it came from because a camel will never get lost.

Occasionally an animal can become so exhausted that there is nothing they can do but slaughter it and eat its meat.

They say that it is a wonderful thing to see when one of the few female camels in the train gives birth to her baby. The train cannot stop so they place the baby on the back of another one and the mother follows close behind her offspring.

It is 60 days of travelling on the back of a camel under the harsh sun of the Sahara with nothing to see except the arid sand of the desert and the other camels that accompany them.

All the guides, fellow travelers and herdsmen start the journey in good spirits, singing, chatting and laughing for a wage of between

600 and 1,000 LYD. The atmosphere in this inhospitable place is always one of camaraderie and helping one another because the nature of the environment makes that essential.

You never know when you might need your fellow companions and it could cost you your life, so mutual support is absolutely fundamental. It is a characteristic of these desert people but even more noticeable in these camel trains where conditions can sometimes mean the end.

The first warning they gave me when I let them know how much I wanted to go with a camel train was that women never travel with them and that my request would not be well received by the guides.

My hope was that, as the groups were in fact independent from each other, if I joined one that would accept me and I kept close to it, perhaps the others would forget about me. At the end of the day, it was a job and everyone had to see to their own duties and responsibilities.

They fondly tell stories about the memory and intelligence of camels.

On one occasion a Libyan bought a camel at the Sabha market and, together with two other camels he had bought earlier, he took them to the Libyan Alhamada for a herdsman to look after them with some others.

The camels had two brands as do all Libyan camels: one for the tribe and the other for the owner.

Periodically, he would return to Alhamada to see his camels until one day he found they had disappeared. He began his search by asking everyone and revisiting all the places where the animal could possible have gone, however, his search was totally in vain.

Little by little, more and more people began to learn of the disappearance of these three camels and, at the end of six months, a man got into contact with the owner saying that he had found two of his camels at a water source north of Niger. The man was astonished at this possibility and took his car and drove to the place. There were his two camels who, on trying to return to their place of origin, had died.

After a time he heard that his third camel had managed to arrive alive at the Nguigmi savannah.

With this story I also want to demonstrate how information crosses the whole of Libya through the tribal network without the need for the media.

The Nomadic Flocks of Sheep

A friend of mine, Mohamed, has a flock of around 50 sheep and several goats. He keeps them on the outskirts of Sabha due to the ease of buying feed, if they need it, and because there are many good wells.

However, when the NATO bombing and siege of the country began, there was no electricity so they could not pump the water from the wells. The animals began to die of thirst. To make things worse, armed gangs who came with NATO, robbed them and the bombs fell daily.

Mohamed decided to take his sheep to al Wadi Shati which, at that time, was a little safer so he travelled some 80 kms across the desert for several days to get there.

Before long, the NATO planes began bombing el Wadi Shati as well and again the armed gangs arrived. Many sheep died from an unknown disease.

Mohamed decided to get away from that area.

He is a man of the desert, capable of finding his way and anything he needs at any point in the Libyan Sahara.

Finally, he decided to move the flock to the Ubari area. He crossed the desert for ten days with several dogs and two of his nine sons, one of seven and the other ten years old.

Along the way, three lambs were born and the mother of one of them died so Mohamed's little boy took care of the baby and carried him in his arms for the entire journey. He fed it with a little goat's milk and a liquid made from dates and water.

One night when Mohamed had gone in search of wood, a group of wolves came in search of a sheep. The boys were very frightened and hid. The dogs barked and tried to keep the wolves at bay but there were too many and they felt very courageous against only two dogs.

Finally, ten days later they arrived in Ubari and Mohamed went straight to a grocery store to buy baby's milk to give to the little lambs and he gave them a lot while his son told him not to give them so much. The three baby lambs died after drinking the baby milk and his son cried for days.

Mourning

The Libyan culture is full of contrasts and the latest modern customs blend in perfect harmony with the most ancestral.

The old people in Libya tell how in the old days when a woman became a widow she would have to mourn for her husband for an entire year. The woman would take refuge in the animal shed and would not wash or change clothes until a year was up.

Then she would come out of the shed and would rub an animal all over her body as part of the ritual for ending her mourning. From then on, she would go back to normal life.

Nowadays, it is possible that many of these customs are not even known to the majority of Libyans. Just thinking about hygiene, it would be unthinkable for a Libyan not to wash himself. I do not know a cleaner people.

Such is the discretion, good manners and respect attached to mourning, that I never had the opportunity to witness any mourning ceremony or the ending of it during my first few years in Libya. I am pleased, however, to have had the opportunity to experience this.

Today, when a Libyan woman becomes widowed, she remains in mourning for four months and ten days and, at the end of this time, there is a ceremony.

The new widow leads a completely normal life within her family and/or tribe. During this time, however, she does not use perfume, go to parties nor does she dress in elegant or party clothes or use henna.

When the four months and ten days are up, the whole family gets together to fete the widow. They put henna all over her body, creams on her skin, perfume, new clothes and they sing and dance.

The ceremony that I experienced was one where the husband had died at 23:30. The wife, therefore, stayed in a room with her daughters and close relatives so they could help her to get ready. She stayed in the room until exactly the time at which her husband had died. Meanwhile, the rest of the family attending the ceremony waited outside and another part of the family prepared the dinner for all those present - around 100 people.

Each tribe has its own characteristic rituals but, in a nutshell, they are all about the END of the period of mourning for the husband's death and from that moment onwards the widow will lead a perfectly normal life.

Sometimes, for example they will postpone weddings and family celebrations during the mourning period. However, if for special reasons a wedding is celebrated before the mourning period has ended, then the wedding will be short and last a maximum of two days instead of the usual five.

In reality, it seems natural and healthy to me that a woman who has undergone the trauma of the death of a husband spend four months in peace surrounded by her family in order to recuperate a little from the experience and from the sorrow that she is feeling.

The rituals to end the period of mourning are tender and moving.

During this special day for the end of mourning, all the women wear white except for the widow who will wear black. From this day on, she can dress in white or in any colour she wishes.

Terfes

From the very first week when I arrived for the first time in Libya, I heard the Libyans talking about the most exquisite food you can find, in their opinion: Terfes. (Terfes come from the same family as truffles).

I heard so often about the marvels of the flavour of the terfes that I began to dream about going to Libya right after the rains to be able to try them for myself and enjoy them.

Quite frankly, I had idealized them too much!

The Libyans will tell you that the terfes are the manna that comes directly from heaven. And the bible talks about this food as the manna that God sent to the people when they had nothing to eat.

Really, it is amazing to see the places where they appear because they are in arid, cloddy parts of the desert where it only rains once a year. In Libya the area where they sprout is to the south of Montes Nafusa on the west side of the road from Tripoli to Sabha. There are hundreds of kilometres of flat land that is arid and sandy.

They grow below the soil together with a certain type of grass and when they appear just a little bit above ground, that is the perfect time to pick them.

Collectors can tell from far away which places will have them and they can find many kilos, especially if there has been a lot of rain.

Once I asked Osama why they did not preserve them to eat throughout the year, if they were so good. He replied that they like them so much there are never any left over.

The first time that I managed to eat them, I remember that I bought them on the road from Tripoli to Sabha on my arrival in Libya. I was travelling the the 800 kms between Tripoli and Sabha by car and there were men by the side of the road with boxes full of terfes.

At the start of the season they are expensive but as the supply increases, then the price goes down and it is always a little celebration when someone brings home terfes.

I was very surprised to see how they prepared them since they are simply boiled in water, peeled and then eaten. That was how they were offered to me the first time and I was surprised and disappointed as I had conjured up this wonderful dream, and the flavour, as well as the simple way of cooking them, made them seem a little insipid to me. It pains me to say this and I hope my friends do not read this.

Later on I ate them in noodles or with cous cous and while my friends spent time savouring each piece of the terfes, frankly I remained unimpressed.

I have read that the Libyan terfes are the best in Africa and that kings in olden times would travel for months from other countries just to eat them. For this reason and because of everything the Libyans said, I am embarrassed to say that I never managed to elevate this food to the heights where history and the Libyans had placed it.

Osama and Ibrahim went to the Alhamada for several days, to the area where they know that the terfes grow, to collect as many kilos as they could and make some money. They left in high spirits and with plans as to how they were going to spend the money they would make. It was like the proverbial Spanish folk tale about the milkmaid who had grand plans for the money she would make from selling milk. She would then buy chickens who would lay enough eggs to buy a new cow and so forth... only to have the milk urn fall of the cart before even getting to market!

What happened is quite usual in Libya and can only be accepted with a sense of humor. Osama told me they had managed to collect 45 kilos of terfes. Right away he had done some mental calculations and thought they would have made around 1,000 LYD (Libyan Dinares) so they should be very happy. However, Osama began his explanation very slowly with many pauses and what happened next happens in all the large tribal families. He returned to the Alhamada and despite the fact that Ibrahim had only driven the car, he gave him half of all the terfes collected. Then, before going to the market, he stopped by his house to say hello to his parents as usual. His father was ill with a chronic ailment and the whole family love terfes, so without hesitation he gave them several kilos. While he was there, his sister closest to him in age arrived. She is married with several children so, of course, Osama gave her a large bag of terfes. Then he went home where his wife was waiting and, as one does, told her to take all the terfes she wanted.

In the end, I can't remember exactly if he managed to sell anything at the market but I realized that he had forgotten all of his initial plans and just felt good. I imagine that his happiness came from knowing that he had given pleasure to a lot of people and he never again mentioned the money that he had lost as we would with our western mentality.

I remember that he told me that they were delicious and that his wife and enjoyed eating lots of them.

Only I remembered his words as he left in search of terfes, when he had plans for the money he would make and what he would spend it on.

Generational Changes

It is evident, and we are constantly reminded, that there are great differences in the way of thinking between parents and children, as much for the changes that are taking place in the world, as for the fact that both groups are in different stages in their development and therefore see life from differing perspectives.

These differences are even more marked in Libya because the generation gap is more of an abyss.

While the family matriarchs of around 70 years old are practically illiterate, had many children, dress in traditional Libyan clothing, married as teenagers, look after the children, lived in adobe brick houses, suffered much hardship and only the strongest survived since medicines and hospitals were rare, the next generation has basic primary and secondary schooling and a great many have begun university studies, live in large, comfortable houses with air conditioning, refrigerators, telephone, television with a satellite dish which allows them to see every channel in the world by simply moving the parabolic antenna according to what they want to watch.

The elderly Libyans, quite differently from our elders whom we tend to put away in seniors' homes, are social creatures, well respected and right in the heart of the family and tribe - with all that that entails.

At the same time, the young people have been brought up by

142

their parents according to classic Libyan culture but have studied and seen on television a world that is completely different which tends towards individualism and a fascination for technology.

University and post graduate studies overseas give them a much broader view of life.

The rules for living together and the great respect for one's elders that exists in Libyan culture means that the two cultural influences blend together creating something unique and very special.

Customary or Unwritten Law

Customs and law function side by side like nothing I have ever seen in the west.

While in the west customary law is becoming increasingly restricted, especially in Spain where only small examples remain, such as the water court in Valencia whose decision is final even over the Supreme Court because, in this instance, customary law takes precedence over written law. In Libya, on the other hand, priority has increasingly been given to the traditions of groups which take precedence over any written law. In these cases, the written law is used to complement such traditions so as to avoid any abuse.

Libyans meet to come to an agreement between parties using the unwritten law that originates from the group. By this, I mean that normally both parties will do everything possible to come to an agreement. They know that if they do not accomplish this, then the written law will come into play and that it is more unfair than any agreement.

Libya has encouraged customary law in order to resolve the constant tribal wars that were formerly waged in the whole of the Sahara in Libya as well as Algeria, Mali etc.

A tribe always had to pay a blood debt, something that provoked terrible clashes which ended up turning into small wars between tribes. Older Libyans remember the danger of going out into the street 50 years ago because there were always clashes or one could erupt at any time.

Little by little, thanks to customary law and preaching the virtues of peace, these violent confrontations between tribes finally ended and more and more marriages began to take place between them.

An example that I remember was of a young man who drank alcohol and while drunk ran over someone and killed them. In the west, the law would intervene immediately in this type of case.

However, in Libya the family of the guilty party will quickly intervene, establishing what happened. They then will try to put themselves in the place of the victim and their family and, after a tribal meeting, they will send representatives to the victim's family accompanied by the person responsible for the accident and, in addition to asking forgiveness, they will try, one way or another, to find a way to make amends for the damage caused. These meetings can last days, weeks or months until the victim's family pardon the guilty party and decide that it had been the will of God that this misfortune took place. The agreement they reach can be one of understanding, forgiveness or monetary compensation. The different types of situations, people who intervene etc. can give rise to many options.

In the old days, if two young men were physically fighting each other, they would next each go and look for their brothers and then look for each other again for another fight. The hatred and vengeance would continue to escalate until something really awful could happen. However, having encouraged customary law, the response of the families of the two young men changed completely. They will get together, will try to clarify what happened and try to get the boys together again in order to resolve the issue without grudges. This practice throughout the years has made the Libyan pacific and prone to dialogue. Furthermore, they themselves have been able to see the results which in turn have been motivational.

More or less parts of the tribe will intervene in these meetings including sometimes even tribal leaders, depending on the situation under discussion.

These debates do not just occur on a personal level between two families or several families in one tribe, or between several different tribes, but also when the government wants to change a law and one or other tribes do not agree.

A few years ago, I experienced something which I have

145

already mentioned in that part of the government and several tribes wanted to change the way the oil profits were handled because the government made the investments, paid the schools, food, taxes etc. However, they had realized that along the way a lot of money was disappearing. For this reason, the government and several of the tribes wanted the Libyans to receive their benefits directly and be responsible for their own expenses. They also said that this change would be beneficial because Libyans were spoiled and not used to being responsible for their own expenses.   This possible change gave rise to all Libyans giving their opinions on each and every option and they took part in the debates in the tribal and government assemblies. Everyone had their own opinion.

All this was explained to me for the first time by a teenager of 14. Frankly, I thought that this young man had a big imagination. How could he know these sorts of things and on such a level? I asked him where he had got all this information and he told me from his father as well as from school. He also told me what his father's thoughts were on the issue.   Despite all his explanations and accustomed as I was to the really bland information we usually receive, the truth is that I thought he was dramatizing it all.

I asked a lot of other people who all said the same thing and each one gave me their opinion, depending on how they saw or felt about it. I then realized that when the town councils or tribal leaders took their votes on the proposals to the government, they were really well informed on public opinion received from family members, friends, neighbours, etc.

Any discussion I might have on politics will never leave my home, however, in Libya, with its huge tribal network and town councils, you have the impression that from the moment someone talks to his wife or brother they are now in that network.

In my experience, I believe that this way of resolving conflicts is more satisfying to the parties, is fairer, and obviously there are fewer people incarcerated, as well as encouraging dialogue and meetings with people instead of confrontations.

All Libyans talk, comment and discuss these topics and family events instead of talking about football.

Osama told me about something that happened 20 or 30 years before during the process of the pacification of the Libyan tribes. Reading carefully we can see the great differences and cooperation between tribes and official Libyan law.

Libyans traditionally have the custom that if a young man marries, then the family will try to have the brothers and sisters of the bride marry with the brothers and sisters of the groom and all within the same tribe, where possible, or with neighbouring tribes. I will tell it exactly as it was told to me by Osama.

"My uncle went to a family to ask for a wife for his own son. After a year and following family traditions, the family should ask for a daughter from that house. For this, my cousin, Mohamed, proposed to a girl in the same family at the same time as a young man asked for the hand of Mohamed's fiancee's sister. This young man was called Khalet. While Mohamed was in a good financial position and was hardworking and well respected, Khalet was very lazy, smoking hashish and penniless. For this reason, when Mohamed went to visit his fiancee, he would take gifts for her sister as well because he knew that Khalet had nothing.

Mohamed is from my tribe, he is a Zwai while Khalet is from the same tribe as the two sisters, a Sherif.

Each time that Khalet went to see his fiancee, her sister spent the entire time protesting that Khalet was not earning any money, did not bring any gold or gifts etc. She was always comparing him to Mohamed who would bring her gold and many other things. Day after day this situation began to cause anger and envy in Khalet and, instead of motivating him to work, in his heart he waqs jealous of Mohamed.

One day Khalet arrived at the house to visit his fiancee and met Mohamed talking to the two sisters. He became so angry that he attacked him and they had a fight. Mohamed was a very peace loving and religious man and really Khalet was looking for an excuse to take out his hatred on him.

When Mohamed got back home, he told what had happened.

147

His younger brother, Nwir, became so angry knowing that good-for-nothing, Khalet, had dared to punch his older brother that he took his car in search of Khalet and found him in the street. He stopped the car and confronted him angrily. The discussion became more heated until it came to using their fists.

It is important to underline that Nwir was from the same tribe as Khalet's mother so there were ties between them and furthermore, Nwir was a good person and very religious. He had no intention of killing Khalet but only to force him to say sorry for what he had done to his older brother.

Nwir was much stronger than Khalet and, on getting involved in the fight, hit Khalet with a pipe. Khalet then took a knife out of his pocket and stabbed him under his left arm directly in the heart.

Nwir was 23 and Khalet around 30 years old.

On seeing Nwir fall, people began to come over to help him and he was taken immediately to the hospital in Sabha. The fight happened in the morning and Nwir remained conscious in the hospital until around 5:00 o'clock in the afternoon when he died from internal bleeding.

While Nwir was in hospital, his older brother Mohamed went to look for Khalet and followed him in the car to run him over. Then he stopped instead went over and punched him. It is important to note that Mohamed is very much stronger than Khalet so that, if he had punched him, he had every chance of winning.

Khalet stopped him, saying how sorry he was and explaining that he had only fought with his brother because he had started it and he had no other choice but to defend himself. He reminded him that he was of the same tribe as his mother and finally Mohamed forgave him and they hugged. At that time Nwir had not yet died.

As Mohamed was embracing him, Khalet took out his knife again and stabbed him three times, seriously wounding him and leaving him immobile on the ground. He was also rushed to the hospital in Sabha.

Libyan law is much more severe if you use the part of the knife for killing than if you use the part of the knife for cutting. Khalet had used the tip for killing which makes him much more guilty in the eyes of the law.

At that same time the problems between the families began, that is to say between the Zwai tribe of the victims and the Sherif tribe of Khalet. When they heard that Nwir had died, things became even more complicated.

The young men from the Zwai tribe began to gather and to arm themselves. By this, I mean all the young men in all areas of Libya who belong to this tribe, such as Ijdabiyah, Benghazi, Al Kufrah etc. They arrived in buses and sent their people in al Wadi Shati to support the victims' family and settle the debt of blood, if necessary.

The police then intervened in the most pacific way possible. The first thing they did was to protect Khalet's family with a police presence to avoid more deaths and to tackle the problem because it is easier to protect a family than to arrest an entire tribe.

The Zwai tribe assembled to try and find a solution and calm down the young men.

The first thing that Khalet's family did was to take him straight to the police and hand him over as a sign of compliance with the law. Despite this, the family did not dare open its businesses or go into the street for weeks, nor pass near a member of the Zwai tribe.

The elders of Khalet's tribe approached two other tribes to be mediators to talk to the elders of the Zwai tribe and ask that they receive them for discussions. In former times they would have to go with the guilty party dressed in white to offer him to the Zwai tribe so that they could kill or pardon him, as they deemed fit. However, Khalet had already been handed over to the police so they went to talk to the elders without him because now a law existed instead of the ancient customs.

They never once asked for pardon during the meeting between

the elders from Khalet's tribe and from the Zwai. What they did do was talk a great deal, recognizing the guilt of Khalet and asked the Zwai to tell the authorities what they had decided.

In the meantime, Khalet's entire tribe living in Wadi Shati, which was around five families, collected their belongings and left the area for several months.

A few days after the incident, the elders from the Zwai tribe met with the elders from the Sharif tribe who arrived at the meeting with a police escort to guarantee the safety of the victim's family and to prevent any more problems arising. Khalet's father spoke recognizing the guilt of his son and said that he understood whatever measures the Zwai might take in view of this terrible situation, but he reminded both tribes that they were bound by blood ties and that he hoped they would remain united. After this meeting the elders decided that everything had been resolved and they should stop and calm down the youths.

Khalet remained in prison for 5 years. Afterwards, Khalet's family went to the family of the victims to ask for pardon for Khalet. This is a very important detail and one which the Libyans see as a game because if the murderer's family had asked for pardon for Khalet from the Zwai, they would not have given it and so the law would sentence him to 25 years in prison. However, on no occasion did they ask for pardon until after the 5 years had passed when the passions and the terrible pain of the death were no longer as strong.

Since the victims' family pardoned him, he was imprisoned for a further 5 years and then left a free man. So, a total 10 years.

When Khalet left prison, his life was not so easy since many people from the family would not greet him, not to mention those from the Zwai tribe.

Throughout this story, based on what Osama told me, we see the tribal elders putting the law into practice.

Always when the law is applicable, they will first go to the tribal elders so that they clarify the situation and give their opinion.

The elders are always going to try to be as fair as possible.

When something happens between two tribes, the police will go immediately to the tribal elders to hear the facts and so that they proceed to mediation because it is the best way to know the truth and to resolve the problem as quickly as possible.

What is more, whenever Libyan law becomes involved, it will take into account the decision of the tribal elders.

I experienced firsthand a conflict in the middle of the Libyan crisis because I knew both families involved and I would like to explain how it played out so that you can form a clear picture of the Libyans still in the middle of such a terrible situation and all being armed.

A person who had behaved in a seriously criminal way sought refuge in the house of a family of his tribe in order to hide.

The family of the victim of this man reproached the family that had sheltered him for not having handed him over to the police or throwing him out.

As those sheltering him did not want to give way and everyone had weapons, the discussions escalated in tone until the victim's family destroyed a car of the family sheltering the man.

This event unleashed a series of acts in which both parties shot at cars, houses, etc. However, nobody was hurt and I know that there was no intention of injuring anyone.

The victim's family, seeing that they kept on protecting the delinquent, burned his house.

At that time there was no police or government to resolve the issue and if they all killed one another, nothing would happen and it would not even make the newspapers. The reality is that the young men from this tribe sought to quickly try and resolve the situation and lower the aggression on the part of both sides, but they were unsuccessful. The tribal elders met, analyzed the facts, gave a verdict that resolved the conflict and everything finished.

1. Due to not being able to hand him over to the police, they expelled the young delinquent who had caused all the problems from the city and from his tribe.

2. They ordered the victim's family to pay for the damage to the burned house because the family of the delinquent was innocent and now had no home.

The two families accepted the resolution of the elders and the confrontations stopped. The two families went on to pardon one another.

They have spent years resolving conflicts, no matter how serious, by means of meetings and decisions from the tribal councils formed by respectable tribal elders or extended family. I understand that someone might worry about corruption when forming the tribal council, however, it is simply that the tribe only accepts the decisions of the most respectable men who have demonstrated throughout their lives that they have wisdom gained from experience and a capacity to relate well to others. At times things are cleared up in a few days, as in this case. Other times, however, many tribes may get involved and it can take several weeks or months because the issues or conflicts can be very different and complicated, as is the case in any part of the world.

Natural Medicine in the Sahara

In Libya there are hospitals in all the towns however small they might be. However, Libya is a country almost three times the size of Spain and there are many kilometers of road crossing through the desert and many people who live on farms (which here we would call 'oasis') many kilometers from the next populated area. Perhaps because of this they have many home remedies for small ailments.

On one occasion we were returning from the city of Ghat on the south east of Libya almost on the Algerian border, towards the Akakos hills and I saw an oasis in the distance, that is to say, a green area in the sand in the middle of nowhere. I asked what that place was and if we could go. They told me that it depended on how many people were there because at times there were too many people. We arrived and saw huge tents erected around a green area with two houses made half from palm leaves and half from stone.

They explained that there were natural springs of medicinal water that were very good for the bones and for this reason entire families of Tuaregs came from Algeria travelling for weeks to bathe in these waters.

I too really wanted to bathe in these thermal springs, talk to the people and spend hours with them. However, in the beginning they looked at us without approaching us because they were not used to foreigners. My friends asked if I could bathe and quickly two little girls took me into one of the two houses. There I encountered a magical scene that I shall never forget. There was a huge square pool made of stone and on one side cascaded a wonderful jet of hot water.

On seeing me come in, the women who were in the pool completely dressed in bright colored clothes that stuck to their bodies, got out of the water and sat relaxing on stone ledge all around, creating a wonderful mental image that I still have engraved on my memory.

One of the women unplugged the drain of the large stone tub and when it was completely empty, they told me to undress and get in.

The truth is that I was dying to get in as much for the experience of it all as for the fact I had come in from the desert sand in the summer in the middle of the day and I was quite hot.

I did not want to take off my underwear even though they kept on insisting because they all bathe completely dressed and they stood around me as if it were some theatrical event and I was the main attraction.

If I was a theatrical event for them, then I have to acknowledge that, for me, they were a sweet vision of loveliness.

I have always been shy regarding these things but frankly I remember feeling completely happy and relaxed dreaming of getting into that bath with its medicinal water. The water was hot, so hot that it was hard to bear the heat on your face. I thoroughly enjoyed being under that large jet of water, sitting on the stone of the huge tub, whilst once and a while looking at the picture of all those women on the ledge around me looking, laughing and making comments.

It was an exquisite picture that I still keep in my mind's eye. We all enjoyed ourselves because they had fun watching, laughing and talking amongst themselves and me, in this surprising bath in such an unusual place, surrounded by women who for me were so exotic and immersed in an atmosphere where I felt completely happy. If I have to think of a moment of happiness in my life, without a doubt I will remember that day in that huge stone bath. At the time I felt that even though I could not capture that image in a photo, it would never be erased from my mind.

The same little girls who had accompanied me to that place, were looking after my clothes and gave them back to me when I got out. They asked me if I could please visit their family. They were

Tuaregs, nomads from Algeria and spoke French and Arabic. I talked to my friends to find out if I should go and they told me it was an honour to be invited to their tent and that I should go and talk to them without any qualms.

I found the tent which was open on one side forming a large

porch and seated there were men, women young and old, children and babies. I sat down and we began chatting in my schoolgirl French but what is certain is that we understood each other.

When I told them that I was a pharmacist, they began to ask me for help because they are desert people and had a few small problems. They asked me if I had any medicine. Fortunately, I had a large medicine chest with me and began giving them what they

asked for from what I had.

At the end of several hours we left. I felt happy, cool and clean. It had been a wonderful day.

I would have loved to have taken photographs of these people, however, they do not like photographs and the only one I managed to take was from a distance as we were leaving and it was only of one of the tents.

The water from the salt water lakes of the Ubari dunes is also used to cure ailments especially those of the skin, most particularly psoriasis. The Ubari dunes sea once was a real sea and there are still traces of small areas of water which they call lakes. There are eleven of them. The most visited is lake Gabroam because of its accessibility. It is the largest and next to an ancient town.

Its water is approximately seven times saltier than sea water. A few metres from the lake is a source of fresh water.

The Algerian Tuareg nomads sell their handmade crafts there and the Libyans have made a bar and small houses to shelter from

the heat and to give a little intimacy to the Libyan families who go there for their treatments and to enjoy a weekend of relaxation.

Next to this lake there used to be a village where many Libyan families lived. Now, however, it is abandoned because the Libyan government built houses close to the Sabha/Ghat road so that they had access to electricity, schools, hospitals, etc.

Someone might look at these simple constructions and think that they exude an air of poverty. Nothing could be closer from the truth as the first thing you have to take into account is that in order to get to this lake you have to cross many dunes which can only be done in 4x4 driven by Libyan experts.

These little adobe houses would be the changing rooms for people where they could change their clothes and leave their belongings while take the waters or sunbathing.

I have enjoyed many happy times at this lake on many occasions because it is a pleasure to swim in water where you will float effortlessly without hardly moving your hands or feet, but you must always take care not to get water in your eyes as the high concentration of salt will make them sting.

It is a heavenly place to relax, sit and eat or drink something, to climb the large dunes and then to slide down them on skis, a board or with the car.

After spending several weeks in the desert, far from any inhabited place, it is very pleasant to reach the area of the great sea of the Ubari dunes and Lake Gabraom to refresh and restore oneself and barbecue a little meat.

Many groups of young people go there at the weekend to have a barbecue and enjoy the area. One time we met up with a group of people who even invited us to eat with them and together we laughed and danced.

It is an experience that I will never forget because since then and every time that I meet one of the young people that were there, they always say hello and even helped me because one day I was in passport control at the airport when one of the young men I had met in Ubari stopped, spoke to the police and they ushered me through the line. Afterwards, the police asked me if I knew him and how I knew him, I had trouble replying and decided to talk little and smile a lot because I remembered his face but hadn't a clue as to his name or where I had met him.

There are also some trees in the desert whose wood is sold in the markets because the Libyan women use the smoke from that wood. They say that it tones up a woman's intimate area after childbirth.

I have read that also in other African countries they use the smoke from this wood and even make special chairs with a hole in the seat so that the smoke reaches the appropriate place. From what I could see, this was nothing strange but something very normal that all married women knew and obviously they offered it to me as well.

I thought it very funny that they were offering me this wood and I wondered why but imagine that, knowing that I am also a mother, thought I would like to "tone up". I took some wood home with me and for a long time it remained on top of the dresser in my bedroom. Each day I thought I should probably try it out and see what I felt and if it worked, but I realized that I should have done it over there because when you take something out of its environment, it is more difficult to do it. "Where should I burn the sticks? How should I sit so that the smoke reaches the appropriate place? Each day I thought about it until one day my sister arrived. I told her about it and she wanted to try it, so I gave her the sticks.

I hope to return to Libya and try it, and then I will add an appendix to the book to tell about the results.

El Bakhur

In Libyan homes they burn Bakhur every day and the aromatic incense penetrates every corner of the house.

In fact, I have never smelled Indian incense in a Libyan house. What this does is it stops the houses from smelling musty or of food.

Every home has several terracotta pots:

In these pots they put charcoal embers and a little Bakhur on them.

Bakhur is the name Libyans give to all sorts of resins, aromatic woods and mixtures of the two that they make themselves by combining woods together with different types of essential oils.

There are shops selling these different sorts of resins, perfume, essential oils, creams and natural products.

In my Libyan home it was always the same person whose duty it was to burn the resins every day and she showed me something funny. They place the pot on the floor and stand over it with their clothing covering it. That way, it has a secondary use: body deodorant.

I am in love with these shops and could spend hours in them. My Libyan friends cannot understand what it is that I want to see or find and they always ask me what I am looking for exactly. I cannot tell them, however, because I do not know. I only want to know what every item is that they have.

Each time I go, I discover something new but I need to ask a lot of questions because everything is written in Arabic.

I like to buy musk tablets to put in cupboards because they are good for getting rid of the smell of damp and keeping away moths. There are many types and they all smell a little different so I am becoming expert on all the different ones. They last forever or at least for as long as I have bought my first tablet many years ago. On the other hand, I bought some tablets in Morocco. They looked the same but hardly had any scent and after several days they did not smell at all. It would seem they cheated me.

I also really liked the smell of some cubes which they called

"ambar" but which does not refer to amber resin. They smell very nice and I would say even better than the musk.

Libyans also refer to nutmeg seeds as "ambar" and say they are the same, however, I believe there has to be some mistake because they do not smell the same.

Libyan women are accustomed to shaking or touching hands when they greet each other so they will rub them with a little "ambar" and then when they extend their hand to someone, the pleasing fragrance is passed along.

The (Eternal) Greetings in Libya

Greetings are formulaic and very long before you actually say anything concrete. For example, women will hug and kiss on each side while both ask each other how they are, how the family is and they name one after the other, how are they doing, if they have got better, if they had been ill, etc. etc. These greetings can go on forever and when it is all over, they will separate and begin to talk.

For a long time I was fascinated by this protocol because I did not understand what they were saying and it seemed a cross between a song and a poem from both people at the same time.

In Libya it is the height of bad manners to meet someone and immediately speak about what you had to ask. Beforehand you must greet, ask how they are, if there is any news and slowly come around to talking about what really interests you.

Said this way, it sounds very good, however, from day to day at times my western culture takes over and I have an idea in my head, I see the person that I am looking for and want to ask them something directly but it doesn't matter because that person will smile, ask me how I am, how is everything and several more introductions until they allow me to get to the question I had for them at the outset.

On the other hand, I found it hard to understand that Osama came to tell me, for example, that his father had passed away but before saying so allowed several minutes of introduction that I had interpreted as an interest in talking about other things before he then tells me something so sad and so important. The same thing happened when he told me that Ibrahim had had a stroke.

From my framework of reference, information is so important and affects you so much that it is difficult to control your feelings and facial expressions until the greetings are over, however, I have seen on many occasions that this is something normal for them and it could be wrongly interpreted from a culture so different to theirs, as is ours.

If I have something to tell a close friend, it would be very hard and totally artificial for me to follow this protocol but I understand, and have been able to confirm, that it is something totally natural to them.

My first Impression of Family Life

In the beginning, when I began to live with the Libyan family, I developed my own ideas of Libyan society, ideas that I feel are important to write down since they could help in some way bridge the gap of understanding between western society and Libyan culture. I dare not say all of Arab culture because I do not believe that you can generalize on such a grand scale, the same as I do not believe that all whites, all Christians or all Europeans are of the same idea or way of life or thinking.

For some reason and always from our western culture, we have made generalizations about "the Arab world" and biases in our interpretation of it that have engendered a rejection of, or a state of alert at least, towards this world. We have been told terrible stories about harems, customs, that men treat their wives as objects and can have as many as they want, about the burkha, removal of parts of the body and about the Koran as encouraging terrorism, etc.

Obviously, on arriving in Libya and without being aware of it, I had also been a little brain washed, so my interpretations were always based, in part, on western prejudices.

Life in the home of my family was very conventional within the framework of their culture, under the influence of traditions to which each member of the family feels a bond, based above all on the Koran. I lived in the south in an area less directly influenced by the outside world.

From a very young age both in the home and at school, children are taught to respect their parents. It is something that you breathe in the day to day behaviour of all members of the family and, on asking them, my friends explained this, with reasoning that could be considered a touch childish.

Farah told me that as a young girl, one day her mother, on

165

seeing her leave to go to school, told her she was not dressed properly and asked her to change. Farah refused to change her clothes despite her mother's insistence. She held firm and finally went to college in the clothes she had decided to wear.

In class, the teacher was talking about the importance of respect and obedience to parents and for this used comparisons and examples so that the children would have a clear understanding. Farah began to cry as she listened to the teacher because she felt guilty at not having listened to her mother that morning.

On leaving class, she ran home and immediately hugged her mother and asked her forgiveness. Now Farah is finishing university and never argues with her mother. If her mother ever tells her that she does not like a particular piece of clothing, Farah will go and change without discussion. She does not debate with herself if her mother is right or wrong but sees it as a question of respect for her. Farah says that it is not that important to her whether she wears this piece of clothing or that and if her mother, who has much more experience asks her to change, then it is no problem for her to do so.

I understand that on reading this simple explanation it may seem that Farah's freedom to choose has been taken away and that simply she has a response to a submission learned during her childhood. This is the obvious explanation from our cultural viewpoint.

However, knowing this girl and her self confidence, her good self esteem, her university career, her dreams and life in general, I can assure you that her behavior towards her mother and father has nothing to do with being submissive. Furthermore, there is a daily dialogue which facilitates closeness, acceptance and mutual respect. For this reason, in these cases where a mother might say something like this, it is understood that they obey for a reason of which at least they should be mindful.

Seen through my eyes, living in the home, I believe that the mother has a huge respect for her daughters and I never saw her stop and make them change their clothes on going out.

What is certain is that they have very traditional ideas on behavior in the street. It is frowned upon to loud uproariously in the street, or eat, or wear flashy clothes. It therefore makes sense that a mother, who wants the best for her daughters, teaches them those rules of conduct that she considers most important.

Once we saw a foreign girl dressed in a way that we in the west would have considered very sexy. She was wearing a tight fitting top with straps that showed off her cleavage, shorts that were so short they showed off the top of her buttocks.

I was enormously surprised by the comments from my young Libyan friends, who I know love the ladies.

Instead of looking at her, they avoided her. I asked them if they liked her and they replied that she was very vulgar. That is to say that this way of dressing was not attractive to them nor the way to go around.

The Libyan girls will do the same things but will use other very different forms of behavior and of course they would never go out in the street without dressing up, the same as the men, who will not wear shorts or short sleeves.

As young children they go to classes to study the Koran and its meaning. They are taught in a natural way and not from a mystical point of view. They learn to respect their older brothers, look after the little ones, pray, keep themselves clean, etc. It is as if the Koran was a compilation of rules on ethics, behavior and social hygiene that has nothing to do with fanaticism.

In addition to personal hygiene, they also look after the cleanliness of the home.

The bathroom is considered dirty and for this reason there are rubber shoes at the door to put on when you go in and take off when you leave. As it is an unclean place, you may not take the Koran in there. This was a little inconvenient for me as I like to take something to read and at that time learning about the Koran was one of my goals.

When they talk amongst themselves within the family, I believe that they exaggerate a lot or embellish their words. However, I would interpret them literally. For example, when Mannar said, "I am going to spend a week in my room studying" and then the next day at midday I saw her get up and busy herself with other things the rest of the day, I asked her about what had made her change. She replied that I must not interpret the meaning of her words 100% like when a mother tells her child "I have told you a thousand times not to do that." Obviously, she has not counted the times she has told him and, if she had, it would probably be much less than a thousand. This, applied to a different world, in a different context, will give rise to even more wrong interpretations.

I think that they viewed me as I view the behaviour of Germans whom I consider "square", "rigid".

When they speak they are always mindful of their religion and family. These are two topics that are inseparable from their persona, however, such an idea, seen from the western point of view, gives the impression of submission or of diminishing the persona. In spite of this, I see them as much more spiritually enlightened and with a much freer and simpler life than ours. Seen from the inside, I think that this is a way of helping family relationships and creating stronger bonds. Everyone respects one another in spite of their differences and unity is one of the pillars in Libyan culture.

It would be absurd to think that everything is magical and perfect, however, what is certain is that, despite any differences, likes, dislikes and disagreements that may occur, the rules of living together contribute to making peace again and the resilience of the family. Whilst in the west the process of individualization and personal narcissism ends in loneliness.

The great difference between Libya and the west stems from their goals. While in the west it is "LIVE FOR YOURSELF", in Libya it is "LIVE FOR THE GROUP".

Libyans are very socialized people, contrary to what might appear to people in the west, because they are capable of following the social norms learned and practised since childhood, even putting them above their own personal interests. While in the west, where we believe we are much more advanced and socialized, in reality, our individualism leads us to breaking many of the rules of living together and entering into conflict with those around us. The result of this conflict is, amongst other things, unhappiness, anxiety, depression, stress, etc.

Seen like this, I began to doubt what is better or to what are we referring exactly when we talk about better or worse.

The ideal would possibly be to take the most positives parts of each one of the cultures and create a culture that is a blend of the two but, clearly, this is an absurd utopia because precisely when two cultures come into contact, not just the good is absorbed but also what is most commercial, since we live in a consumer society which influences our lives, starting with MacDonalds or plastic surgery. For this reason, the opening of Libyan culture to the western world will lead to consumerism and the use of "gadgets" to occupy ourselves and will substitute people and conversations. The children already talk about Nintendo, Playstation and play with mobile telephones and watch television. It is clear that consumerism is now a part of Libyan society and as a result, sadly, will possibly go on to replace personal relationships with relationships with things.

When we explore more deeply each one of these people, they too, as is natural, have their own personal goals, dreams and desires just like anyone anywhere in the world. Although they live with their focus on the family and it might appear that they cannot escape the rules, in practice, each person has his own strong, inner freedom and will always find a way to reach his goals.

From the west, we only have negative caricatures of their way of life that make them seem male chauvinists or fanatics when this is far from the truth.

It is funny to see that they make these same mistakes when looking at the west. In some cases they admire us but in others they see us totally as caricatures. Knowing these points of view helped me to understand our responses. It is a little like north Americans thinking that all the Spanish dance flamenco and everyone plays the castanets or when the told me that Spielberg visited Spain and brought with him his own bottled Evian water from the U.S. and asked if Spanish women could go to university.

Every rule of conduct originates in the Koran because it is a book whose purpose is to provide rules of mental and physical hygiene to a society. In order to understand and test this idea, I tried to study the parts of the Koran that gather together these rules. From my studies I can prove that the fact that the women in Saharan and other hot places cover their heads and occasionally their faces, has nothing to do with the Koran but with the climate. The men also cover themselves for the same reason.

The roles in the south of Libya and within this very traditional life are shared and at first very clear. The women look after the house and children while the men undertake tasks outside of the home. However, this is all changing at lightning speed just like the same society. From the moment that the women have a further education, this translates into marrying after 25 years of age, the need to drive, go out, work and, as a logical consequence of this, is a sharing of the work in the home.

The rapid changes in Libyan society have been noticeable

from day to day over the past 10 years.

A clear example is the number of children in my Libyan family. While the matriarch had 15 children, they all have a maximum of three children each.

In my family 15 children have gone to university and the majority have finished their further education, while they live in the most traditional way in the south of Libya. They have been educated to respect their parents and in the rules of conduct set out in the Koran. However, they know the ways of the west. The young people dress in western style and know how to match colours tastefully, while the older people still dress in traditional clothing, depending on their age.

The men in the family wear jeans with a shirt or polo shirt and other days will wear white pants covered with long white tunics called "Xibalas" The traditional dress is generally worn on a Friday when they go to the mosque to pray. Frankly, I think it suits them much better than western clothes.

Los trajes normales que usan las mujeres libias casadas dentro de sus casas

Trajes típicos de las mujeres tuaregs de Ghat y Ghadames

Traje normal mujeres mediana edad para salir a la calle

Vestimenta mujeres mayores

Los niños visten al estilo occidental, como las adolescentes y jovencitas

The side of the family living in Tripoli or in cities in the north always wear western clothes. I have also seen many girls up north who do not even cover their heads anymore. At the moment there is a huge selection of ways to dress which reflects the enormous influences and changes that are taking place in the country since the U.S. lifted its embargo and they could open up to the western world.

I would say that, depending on what part of Libya you are in, you could think you were either in the west or in the middle of the Sahara as much for the way of dressing as for the buildings, shops and streets.

The word "respect" is used a great deal in Libya. It has, however, many more nuances in its meaning than what we give it. For example, when they talk of respect towards man, they are referring to the traditional affection and dedication to family. As an example Khadija would tell that she adored her father so much that many times she would sit at his feet listening to him when he talked but, out of respect, she never dared to raise her eyes to him. Khadija is now 75 years old.

I asked her if her father was hard on her and she replied that he loved her very much and never raised a hand to her. Khadija, therefore, talks of a type of respect we, nowadays, have never known. Khadija now has 15 children and a familiar way with them and, of course, they respect her very much. However, they always look her in the eye and speak to her directly.

Khadija still observes many classical rules of behavior in her house even though not one spoon is moved without her consent.

When they talk of respect, it is always from wife towards the husband, the children towards their mothers and fathers and the younger siblings towards the older ones.

The word "respect" can mean "obedience", "observance of rules and regulations", "consideration", "affection", "correct behavior according to tradition" and also our concept of respect.

I am sure I am leaving out a few things on translating them into English because it is also considered disrespectful to dress in an unseemly way. Anyone can dress as he sees fit, however, it is frowned upon to dress immodestly, by this I mean showing off legs, shoulders etc. and this applies just as much to men as to women.

I have seen western women in bikinis on the beaches of Tripoli or in the middle of the Sahara in the lakes at the Gabraon sea of dunes. Nobody says anything to them but if one of them is looking to be admired, she is mistaken in her way of going about it.

The Libyan men view these women as if they were doing something in bad taste. Libyans are very respectful so they would not make any comment on it, least of all in front of me because, at the end of the day, I am a westerner. After spending so much time with them, they have ended up telling me what they think and I have noticed it. I watched Libyans lose their heads over blue eyes but never over a woman showing too much flesh.

This cannot be seen as a prejudice but as a way of dealing with feelings according to tradition.

On another level, in Spain there were many misunderstandings when tourism began and the tall, blonde, blue-eyed Swedish girls were prepared to sleep with a Spaniard without love or commitment ever entering into the equation. The interpretation that the young people put on this was that these girls were ready to go with "anyone" and that sex to them meant nothing, that they were "easy". They dehumanized them as objects to be used and abused. With many nuances and except for a few differences, much the same thing happens when some more traditional Libyan men see the western women dressing in a flashy way with very little clothing and showing affection to men in public.

The Libyans love and feel just like westerners, however, they reserve those feelings for the privacy of their homes, a little like the English. For this reason, some misinterpret the behavior and body language of some western women in public.

It is very important, however, to clarify that I have never heard a negative comment in public on a situation of this nature. Since Libya opened up to tourism, you would see western women in bikinis and I never heard anyone say anything to them. Many Libyans even had two ways of looking at people because they already know that foreigners are very different. It is a way of viewing them that I understand very well because it is something that we have always felt in Mallorca when we see the tourists on our beaches, on our streets. They do things that we would never do but we know that "they are guiris". For example, it is unthinkable that a Mallorquin would walk down Jaime III street in a swimsuit, however, I have seen more than one tourist do this. Also it would also be unimaginable to see a group of young drunk mallorquins making a scene in the streets of Magaluf. This is done by the guiris, so nobody says anything except when they cause some sort of trouble. There are many things that only the tourists do and we do not even judge them by our own standards because "they are tourists". They can get away with it.

The above is a photograph of two girls swimming in Lake Gabraon in 2009.

I do not know if I am expressing myself with sufficient clarity but what I want to say is that, even on this level, there are many misinterpretations from both sides, that is by Libyans of the westerners and vice versa.

Furthermore, I have seen that on initiating certain types of negotiations with Libyans who are not used to dealing with westerners, many times both parties will break them off and not continue due to a lack of understanding as regards misinterpretation of the behavior of both sides. Friends of mine have asked me at times to help them understand a dialogue with westerners and when I talk about understanding, I am not referring to the words.

The first time I went to Libya on a cultural visit as a tourist, I knew that they had forbidden the desert guides to talk to us westerners and we were told to be cautious of the desert guides as they did not like tourists and to try and avoid any problems, leading us to surmise that they could be dangerous. Nowadays I know these guides, I know their families and I know how they think, and I wonder where anyone got that idea and why this type of behaviour is encouraged which gives rise to the worst types of misunderstanding.

I even knew that one of those guides was a pharmacist and probably had more land, family and homes than most of us. He was born in the ancient city next to Lake Gabraom and knows the desert

like the back of his hand. He is even able to find his way in the middle of a sandstorm when you cannot see half a metre in front of you.

Once there was a group of foreigners who had to get to Sabha airport to fly to Tripoli in a few hours but a terrible sandstorm prevented any visibility and several 4 x 4s had crashed on going up and down the dunes on their way to Sabha as they crossed the Ubari sea of dunes. They were forced to stop until the guide told them to put one car behind the other and follow him. Little by little, without seeing a thing he guided the procession to Sabha without a problem. This is a great feat that the desert people love to talk about and I can confirm that it is true because I personally know those who were involved.

This fear of the unknown, of becoming separated or lost, is very negative because it means that we can never know the truth and we leave the country without ever having really known the true essence of Libya, the Libyans.

Their knowledge puts them on the same level as "desert sea

wolves" because they fix any breakdowns, find water and know the entire Libyan Sahara without needing a GPS. They are capable of resolving the most complicated problems and climbing the most difficult dunes which would seem impossible if you had not experienced it, etc.

The dunes have one slope seen from the car, but you never know how steep they are on the other side because it depends on the wind and many other things. On occasions what appears to be a small dune once crested, can be a precipice on the other side and for this reason, the 4 x 4s must always stop at the top to see what awaits them before going on down. Sometimes, depending on the type of sand, the car can get stuck.

With all of this, I mean that the people are experts and multi-talented. They have capabilities gleaned from living their entire lives in the Sahara that would be very hard for a westerner to ever acquire. Of course, it is their environment.

Despite the lack of trust from some westerners, the desert guides are people born in the Sahara and therefore people who live for the group and who would be capable of giving their lives for the people in their charge. The tourists leave without realizing up to what point they could have trusted in them and possibly in the west have no friend that would be deserving of so much trust.

The only time in all my years visiting the Libyan Sahara that the car broke down was after a terrible sandstorm, the worst I have ever experienced. I remember that we were in a large plain in front of the highest dunes in the Sahara on the Massif of Murzuq. The wind was so strong that we could not see anything but sand around us. Osama stopped the car and calmly said "that's it". He placed his bare feet on the seat, as they are used to doing. It was midday and very hot so that being inside the car was really unpleasant. I took a large piece of lightweight material and wrapped myself in it. I then got out of the car and stretched out on the sand covered by the cloth. In the beginning it felt as if my whole body were being pricked by needles but I very quickly got used to it. Furthermore, after a while a friend came and lay beside me and together we began to talk and talk until we wondered what had become of the car and our friends. They had done the same thing as us but under the cars.

I do not remember how long it took but I have a wonderful memory of those hours spent because I remember feeling completely safe in the middle of nowhere in a storm. I was very relaxed talking of things I no longer remember.

When the storm abated a little, the sand had got into the car's engine and an irreplaceable part was damaged which prevented us from going any further.

Nothing happened. They never raised their voices or cursed, nor did I note any sign of tension. Ibrahim and Osama climbed a dune, talked for a while and then after a bit came back and told us that Ibrahim would go and get help from an oil well camp that was relatively close by and that in the meantime we would have some tea and prepare the evening meal, just as if this sort of thing happened all the time and everything was completely normal.

Thanks to the pleasant atmosphere in the middle of nowhere, we drank tea, chatted, laughed and felt happy, as the time passed, it became dark and in the end when it was already night, we saw a light in the distance. Osama, that is, saw a light from far away. We could not see it until much later. The camp was around 20 kms from our position and it took hours for them to arrive and I wondered how they could have known in what direction to go and where the camp was and then come back to exactly the same place where the car was stuck in the dunes. I know for sure, because I was there, that they did not use a compass or GPS or anything like that. When the truck arrived, they greeted us and immediately hooked up our 4 x 4 to their truck in order to tow us, treating us like guests. The truck took us to the camp so we could sleep there for the night.

What does it mean to be the guest of a truck driver in the desert? This is how we all felt from his behavior. He towed us for kilometres and kilometres through areas made flat by the trucks so they could cross the desert between Sabha and the wells in that area.

The driver stopped often to offer us a drink, snack, cold water from his water container to refresh us and, as if this were not enough, he stopped at lunchtime and cooked some Libyan noodles for us that were finger licking good.

An unforgettable and gratifying experience of the only time when we were unable to fix the car and continue on our way.

The Great Libyan Tribal Network

Libya and the entire Sahara are inhabited by tribes.

Possibly due to the difficulties of their surroundings, the desert people have always been very close and have created ties that not only bind the immediate family but also the extended family. This large family which follows paternal family lines, is the Libyan tribe that has nothing to do with the concept of a tribe understood in the west.

The members of the tribes or family groups are not inevitably always close to each other because as they gradually grow larger, their economic interests, needs and adventurous spirit or some other circumstance, have meant that people from the same tribe have dispersed throughout other parts of Libya. And, the larger the tribe, the easier it is to see this, to the point that they even create groups within a tribe that end up becoming a sort of subtribe.

For example, Osama's tribe has family in Benghazi, Tripoli, Al Kufrah, Sabha, Wadi ash Shati and so forth. However, most of them maintain a family home in their place of origin, that is to say in Seva, in Wadi Shati which is the original place that the first members of the Al Zwi tribe came from. It was a man with his wife and six sons who all remain buried in Seva in Wadi Shati. From them the actual Al Zwi tribe was born and grew and spread out.

The leader of the tribe is generally an elder and the person who is considered the wisest. On some occasions a father will turn responsibility over to a son but normally wisdom, good character and an ability to resolve issues are what prevail. He is very respected because of this. Once he has been elected leader, all the members will revere him and his decisions are even taken into consideration by the government.

Formerly, about 50 years ago, marriages were agreed between

families and always within the same tribe. Couples were even determined when children were born and they grew up with the idea that a certain girl or boy would be the woman or man who would be their companion for the rest of their lives. Both the family and those around knew that this couple was betrothed and the union was respected.

When the day of the wedding arrived, the whole tribe would help with the construction of an adobe house for the new family. These guests were given food over the several days it took to build the new home. The inside of the home was the responsibility of the bridegroom.

The bridegroom would give a quantity of gold to the bride which she would keep as insurance and as a sign of her status. The amount of gold depends on each tribe and even on each family but the closer the blood ties between the couple, less gold needs to be given by the bridegroom. If they are cousins, he does not even have to give her any gold.

Cousins would take preference over anyone else when it came to asking for the hand of a girl.

Once the marriage had been celebrated, the bride would go to her new house on a horse and only the husband could help her down.

In those days disputes between tribes made each tribe very tight knit and they would endeavour to keep their members within it.

When the tribal peacemaking process began in the whole of the Libyan Sahara giving precedence to customary law over written law, little by little the tribes began to open up and its members began to marry into other tribes thus creating a huge family network that is impossible to imagine.

In order to understand the concept of a tribe, you need to understand the Libyan world very well which bears no resemblance to our society. The first difference is that each person lives for the group which is exactly the opposite to us as each day we become more and more individualistic.

My Libyan family, as I have already indicated, is made up of a mother, a father and fifteen children, 12 of whom are already married. Due to their studies and jobs, the children live in different parts of Libya but are in frequent contact by telephone, visits and gatherings in Seva so that everyone knows everybody's business and they experience family situations very closely. All of this implies huge advantages as well as disadvantages that can be difficult to resolve. The immediate family would be the married children and their children.

However, the father's brothers and their children and grandchildren are also considered part of the immediate family because they are part of the tribe and you could continue going further back and there are many more members of the tribe, some of whom they may not necessarily know.

Tribal ties bring people together in every sense of the word because, if one of the members goes to another place, whenever they are introduced, the first thing they ask is what tribe they belong to and this pigeon holes each person and then, if they are of the same tribe, they will be invited home and helped in every way necessary as if they were a brother.

Many issues are resolved through the tribal networks that could never be resolved otherwise and they are the best source of accurate and direct information than anywhere else.

The tribes have a Council of Elders and a tribal leader who make all the important decisions on the customary law or any other type of situation affecting the members. These people meet whenever the situation requires and remain in session until they reach a solution to the problem.

I have seen for myself situations where the Council of Elders has intervened and I have been impressed because it is important to be able to count on people with experience, knowledge, memory of the group's history, wisdom, open mindedness and with the desire to resolve problems and with influence on the group. This leads to a more just and human resolution to issues than with the application of our laws. In western culture the elderly are marginalized and along with them, experience and wisdom are ignored, thus losing our current western society that balance which the elderly bring.

The Council of Elders does not meet alone and in isolation to the rest of the tribe instead it keeps them informed, inviting people to give their opinions. They talk with everyone necessary and listen to both sides. The result may take time until they come to the most satisfactory solution possible.

The blood ties mean that the law is never cold or unjust.

The Libyan Tribes

We have already explained throughout the book the real concept of a tribe in Libya, that it has nothing to do with the western concept of "tribe" because we are talking about extended families where people live for the group.

Blood ties are the basis of the social structure in Libya, while in the west this is being increasingly taken over by other institutions so that they no longer play the role of structural support to society.

The Libyan tribes follow the blood lines of the father in order to maintain their name, however, they also have a close relationship with the family of the mother.

It is such a different society to the western one that anything can be misinterpreted or biased intentionally or unwittingly.

For me, it is relatively easy to understand the changes in the past few years thanks to my friends who are over 40 and therefore have experienced this change in Libya, starting from when the tribes were in constant and never ending conflict because there were blood debts to be repaid.

Osama talks about when he was little and the city of Sabha was the most dangerous in the world and even young boys were always spoiling for a fight . However, now that I know him well, I know he is the most conciliatory and peace loving person I have ever met.

He has experienced many things through which we can see how different and hard life was when he was a boy and how it gradually changed to become this society forming a huge peaceful and hospitable tribal family network.

The last tribal war in Wadi Shati took place within the

Hasawana tribe which is the largest in the wadi together with the Mijarha tribe.

A group of families who lived with their houses joined together all from the Hasawana tribe began an argument about something Osama no longer even recalls. The argument became more heated, turning physical and escalating between the members of the two families until one of them died. From this moment and for the next 5 or 6 days the two families fought bitterly and many people died.

Nobody could stop them. The police tried to stop the clashes but failed.

One night after 6 days of continuous fighting, when everyone was asleep, the army suddenly arrived with helicopters, trucks and cars to the area where the families lived. They took everyone from the two families, the elderly, children, women, young men, without allowing them to collect any belongings, to a small village in the middle of the desert. They left them there and told them on no account could they leave. The army then surrounded the village so they could not flee.

They were left with nothing except the clothes on their backs in the middle of the Libyan Sahara in some houses that they were told would be theirs from now on.

The next day army trucks came to the village with food supplies, mattresses and blankets and everything necessary. Everything was new since they could not return to their homes or weapons.

In the meantime, the army went to their homes in Shati and confiscated their weapons.

The feuding families lived in this little village completely isolated and without the possibility of fighting or assaulting each other. They all belonged to the same tribe, that is, they were family and had once loved each other. Little by little, they began to reconcile until at the end of a year the government allowed them to return to their homes to see if they had forgotten their former grievances and had re-established their former affectionate relationship.

From that moment onwards the Shati tribes never fought with each other again.

It was a magnificent lesson that not only helped the Hasawana tribe but also all the families of Wadi Ash Shati who experienced this.

Each tribe has its history known to all of its members since it is the history of their family, its roots, and is passed on from father to son. All Libyans know where they come from, what their ancestors did and where their relatives are.

Osama belongs to the Zwai tribe, so I asked him to give me the history of his tribe and it went like this:

Around 500 years ago the Al Kufrah oasis in the south of Libya near the border with Chad, was inhabited by an Egyptian tribe called Kafrah which means "oasis" in Egyptian. These were peace loving people who cultivated the land and kept animals. They were farmers and knew nothing about fighting.

A few kilometres away, to the north east, in the city of Tazurbu lived the Tbu tribe. They decided to take over the al Kufrah oasis because it was rich.

The Egyptian tribe was not prepared for a fight so they moved to the north to the areas that were more populated in order to find help. They arrived at Ajdabiyah in the north east of Libya in the Sirte Gulf where they asked the Zwai, Marad, Mijaba, Frajin and Al Forjan tribes for help.

The Zwai decided to help the Egyptians in exchange for half of their palms and harvests.

The Zwai tribe is relatively small so in turn they asked for help from the Al Forjan tribe offering them one branch of dates from each of their palms. The Al Forjan tribe agreed and this verbal contract stands to this day.

So, in the great oasis of Al Kufrah, half of the palms would belong to the Al Zwai and these in turn would give a branch full of dates from each of their palm trees to the Al Forjan.

After arriving at this agreement, 400 men from the Zwai tribe from the Ajdabiyah area and some 100 men from the Al Forjan tribe joined up with 2000 men from the Egyptian tribe living in the Al Kufrah oasis.

Half of the men from the Zwai tribe died on the first night of fighting with the Tbu, as well as many Egyptians and several Tbu. It was obvious, however, that many fewer Tbu had died.

After two days of clashes, the Egyptian tribe decided not to continue fighting as they were peace loving farmers and came to the conclusion that it was not worth dying. However, the Libyans from the Zwai and Al Forjan tribes decided that, after all that they had lost, they were not prepared to leave things as they were and give up, so they decided to continue defending the oasis.

In the end, they managed to stop the Tbu and won even though 100 more men from the Zwai tribe died and some 20 from the Al Forjan tribe. They managed to win because they asked for help from other tribes.

Once the Tbu had been subdued, the Zwai tribe stayed on in the oasis of Al Kufrah.

One day, a long time afterwards, a shepherd and his sister were looking after their flock when some men arrived from the Tbu tribe. They killed the young shepherd and kidnapped his sister, taking her to Tazirbu where they lived. The Zwai gathered together and armed themselves to go to Tazirbu and once there kill all the inhabitants and free the young woman who had been kidnapped.

The tombs of an entire town killed by the Zwai still remain in Tazirbu. It was an entire town, men, women and children.

History never forgets.

After this encounter, there were very few Tbu left; only a few in Srua.

The Saharan Rains

In the Libyan Sahara it only rains once, or at the most twice, in one year. When it does rain, however, it can be so intense that it can become a danger.

Libyans are not used to rain, so when it rains it is a huge cause for celebration. Many young people take advantage of the sand when it is wet as it is harder and regular cars can now go on the dunes for a little craziness. They go on the sand to play in the dunes in the cars, going up and down with no experience and with cars that are completely unsuitable. They don't know, nor do they want to know, how dangerous this is and that you need a lot of technical know how to do it. Inevitably, there are many car accidents during the rains.

Normal cars cross the wadis (old river basins) while it is raining and some are swept away by the flood waters. People also drown or are injured by rocks carried along in water.

The lack of experience and infrequent nature of the rains means that some Libyans or immigrants living in adobe houses can be taken by surprise as the houses collapse in the rain which can be deadly, above all in the Murzuq or el Wadi Shati areas where many immigrants come from Niger or Chad.

Places so dry and wonderful like Wadi Mathandush have

drawings carved into the sides of their rocks for a 7 km stretch.

The work of the Libyans living in these areas at a time when there were once lush woods and wadis full of water, show the old ways of life and the animals that roamed there such as crocodiles, ostriches, lions and elephants. After the annual rains, for several days the wadi becomes a flowing river again, recalling its history.

Libya, a Country of Fossils

Whenever we would go on family outings, we would try and find sea horse fossils and it is considered an enormous achievement if someone found one.

My surprise and admiration knew no limits the first time that Osama showed us so many fossils and such extensive areas full of fossils in Libya.

The desert is like nature in the nude. For this reason, it permits us to observe much more easily the passage of time, history, culture and the remains of primitive civilizations, the composition of the earth and beauty in its purest form.

It is something that makes you reflect on how much the geography of the world has changed and, in particular, that of Libya over the years. One of the times that we went from Tripoli to Sabha, the family of one of Osama's sisters travelled with us with two small girls. This meant that we had to stop quite often to stretch

our legs, allow the toddlers to play a little, eat and attend to their needs.

During one of these stops about 400 kms south of Tripoli, in the desert, Osama showed us an area full of marine fossils which was tangible evidence that the sea had once reached there one time in history.

It is also wonderful to visit the fossilized wood in Southern Libya in the middle of the Sahara. It is in the area of Emssack or on the road to the Oasis of Ghadames and Al Awainat.

Or also in several areas of the Akakos hills.

Islam and Mohammed

Religion in Libya is something that is a huge part of society and a normal way of life. All the children know, as if it were a fairytale, the story of the Prophet Mohammed.

From the point of view that I observed in the Libyan families, there is a huge difference with respect to the Christianity that I have experienced in Spain.

To the Libyans, their religion is not a burden and they live it with joy and with more self esteem before God (Allah). That is to say, they do not confess or do penitence, nor are they told that if they die in sin, they will go to hell and things like that which have left a mark on many young Christian believers. Libyans can always count on Allah's mercy, that he will understand and forgive them.

They feel a brotherhood with Christians and Jews since they all believe in the same god and respect other religions. They believe that Mohammed was the last prophet who came to earth to remind us of the teachings that the Prophet Jesus had already given.

I have tried to study and analyze the rules of life that Islam establishes in the Muslim communities and they are rules regarding hygiene and health for the Arab environment in which they are born. At the same time, I can confirm how wrong many of us westerners are with regard to Islam and all the falsehoods that go around that have nothing to do with the truth.

I hope that my story has interested you. I have experienced many wonderful times in Libya that I shall never forget. The country, however, that I knew and loved no longer exists. Friends and relatives of friends have been killed and Libya destroyed.

This book seeks to pay homage to Libya and especially to the Libyans I have attempted to build a bridge to the Libyan culture and its people.

APPENDIX

It is with great sadness that I must add this appendix to say that my dear Osama was murdered.

He was not my husband, son or brother, however, I felt very close to him.

I spoke to him on Wednesday, 22 January 2014 as I have done every day for many years. Later I received a message from him around three o'clock in the afternoon in which he asked me to call. When I called him around seven o'clock, his telephone was off and never back on ever again.

Osama disappeared that afternoon of 22nd January and was missing for an entire week until January 31st when they found his body beaten from head to toe and with a bullet in the chest and another in the head.

During those 8 days we had held out hope of finding him alive and had done everything possible to locate him since in Libya at the moment there is no rule of law or government and murderers roam freely.

On Saturday, 31st January, the family and friends of Osama buried him without being able to wash him or say a proper goodbye due to the advanced state of decomposition.

A scholar of the Koran told the family that they should not weep for Osama because he had died in such a terrible way that for Allah all his sins had been washed away and he was as pure as a newborn child, and most assuredly Allah had placed him in a privileged place together with the prophet Mohammed.

Osama always told me that he did not fear death and that I needed to learn not to fear it since it was simply "a change of rooms". I always replied that I could not feel the same way because I still had many things I wanted to do in this world before I left it. He always laughed and told me that this decision is in the hands of Allah alone.

I hope and wish with all my heart that all his beliefs are true and that now he is happy wherever he may be because he deserves it.

You will always be in my heart, dear Osama.

-¿Keife Hal?

-Ana quais. Keife hal anta?

-Quais al hamdulilla

-Where are you?

-I'm on the farm, I have come to take care a little the animals and the house because we can not leave them so long time alone.

Thieves go to all the farms and houses and you know they have been here three times already in the last year

-It's very dangerous right now that you come here alone. Where is your family?

-They are all now in Wadi Shati because they are not safe in Sabha with all is happening in this moment. But its enough talking about me and sad things. Please lets talk about good things
What are you doing ?.

- I just come back from swimming and I'll do the cooking for my family lunch. But first I have an appointment for a therapy, so I have to close. Just wanted to know how are you and how everything is going on.

- No, please do not hang up, I would like to talk. Now I have a free moment and I'm here alone on the farm. You know I'm always busy at work or with the kids and I can talk now.

- I'm sorry Osama, but I'm late already. I will call you at seven p.m. and we can talk as much as we want.

- You told me that you want I tell old Libyan stories ?. I told you, I've been reading some more stories in a book that my father made me remember that we had when I was little.

- Yes, Osama, makes me really happy, but now I hang fast.

- oooookkkk ... hope we will have the chance to talk again...

I hung up the phone very fast and ran because it was already late. As absurd thought why he said that later perhaps he could not talk to me as he is alone in the farm. I hope he do not ever go downtown to Sabha

Sabha right now with clashes taking place. I wondered, along the way to my therapy work, why he had said these words to me like maybe we would not have any other chance to talk. My mind told me that it was only a innocent game to make me stay longer on the line.

I could never imagine that this was the last conversation I would have with him.

Osama was full of life, in love with his two sons, as I have never seen a man with an exaggerated sense of responsibility for his family.

About three noon I received a message from him in which he said to me, "Where are you?". It was a way of telling me to call him, but I was giving lunch to my family and I thought I would call him later in the afternoon. Anyway he was alone in the farm.

... It happened again in my head his last words. "Hopefully we can ..."

In the afternoon I received a call from Mannar, hir sister,

200

who asked me if I knew anything about Osama because someone had warned them that he had been kidnapped.

Over the past three years, on many occasions I have feared for his life, I have often thought that he might have missed something because he was not responding to telephone or because it was "mukfel" (closed in Arabic). But little by little I feel like he was immortal, despite the terrible situation in which he was immersed.

I knew when they bombed and had to take his family to hide in the desert using tents.

I knew when they bombed power plants, phone, TV, and not let them get food. They spent the whole day just to find water to drink or a few liters of gasoline.

I knew when Misratah went to Sebha with blacklists to capture people. He, along with other young, went to talk to them because there was no aggression in his life. But, he told me, that when he looked into their eyes knew there was no way to talk. "His gaze was empty" with weapons of all kinds.

I knew when the "rats" went to Sabha to impose the tricolor flag by weapons and they met them to tell them that there was no need to fight because they could put the two flags together.

Osama was a man of the desert, hospitable, white soul. He lived the moment and always trusting in Allah.

I heard many times that he was in danger, but always emerged unscathed from the situation.

He told me I will die young because every day things happened that I I can die, like a bullet that today have passed close to me without knowing where it it was coming from. Possibly a stray bullet.

-I have no fear of death

-Come on Osama, I am afraid of death, because there are still too many things I want to do in this life

-Death is like change rooms Leonor, you need not fear. Only

Allah decides when you have to die.

However slowly I lost the fear that something would happen to him and that Wednesday January 22, 2014, when his sister told me her fears I replied that I just talk to him a few minutes ago and he was perfectly. I told him that perhaps he had closed the phone just for a nap.

Mannar thanked me for my words soothed because she was so scared.

But a few hours later she call me again to confirm that he had been captured and the people who told them said that they were green people. He told me that someone had seen that Osama was with Yousef (a neighbor) and some armed men had abduced them.

I accepted the explanation for a week because green Libyans rose up against the government of NATO and alqaeda and were controlling the city of Sabha.

Osama spoke with everyone because he said that "we are all Libyans and we are brothers, we can not fight among ourselves for ideas". Thus, despite knowing that Yousef was a traitor and that the family did not like to talk to him, was not surprised that he had been talking to him. Nor was it strange that he had been captured by green as Osama was talking to him, also he had caught.

We were all very worried but no one feared for his life because the greens can arrest but they are not murderers.
It was to find out where he had been taken.
Then the brothers, friends and family began searching because there is no law in Libya, nor police where to turn, since NATO gave the coup and criminals, extremists, mercenaries and psychopaths are free to do whatever they want.

From my heart, it was even reassuring to know who had captured him, the Green Resistance and I thought that when they will release him I would shoud him because he was near Yousef and have gone to the farm in a so difficult moment without thinking of the dangerous

Days passed with great concern for the whole family. Two of his brothers tried to find him talking to many people concerned.

Two days later Yousef was back to his house, the neighbor who had been captured with Osama.

All his face was bruised and his family and him gave an explanation that initially was accepted by everybody. He said he had been captured by the Greens, who covered their eyes, tied them and took them. Then they beat them and beat them while Osama told him that he had recognized the people who beat them. Then, still in the words of Yousef, they were separated, and never again heard from Osama.

The justification for which had freed Yousef, he said, was because the kidnappers had demanded a financial reward and weapons and his father had delivered.

All very strange because nobody asked anything for Osama. They said they had hidden from Osama and did not release him because he had recognized them and they were afraid. They could not kill him because everyone knew he was being held.

I talked to a general of the Libyan resistance and sought to Osama by all prisons in Libya. After several days told me that they did not have Osama and had not caught him. He said that at this time was completely impossible for anyone dared within its ranks to ask for a reward .Yousef was lying. He recommended go back to Yousef and ask him again because for sure he know a lot more than what he said.

On Thursday 30th someone phone Osama family saying that surely the next day everything would be resolved and Osama would be released. Since these talks had happened several times, but after the call, the person disconnected the phone and managed to not continue.

On Friday January 31th The same anonymous calls the family to say that Osama is in jail in the Tbu in Murzuq, south east of Sabha. The family has finally direct hopes of seeing Osama soon.

In the afternoon a militia found the lifeless body of Osama

close to the place that had been kidnapped along with two more bodies. They took him to the hospital where the forensic anatomical Sabha service says that most probably he was killed the same day he was captured.

He was beaten all over his body, shot in the chest and once in the head. His eyes were not covered and there were not signs that could show that have been and his hands were not bound but were covering his face.

His body was in an advanced state of decomposition so the family could not wash or see him. Only his brother Omar had to go to identify him.

These data clearly show that Yousef lied throughout his explanation.

We now know that was captured to be killed by these groups of mercenaries.

Osama was very brave, intelligent, fast and very creative and for sure it was not easy to catch him. So many people think that really Yousefr was wounded from fighting against Osama defense until they managed to pin him to death and then topped.

The family is so affected that they do not want to see Youse that remains free, so they are thinking about selling their house in Sebha and the farm where Osama was captured and lived with his wife and children.

A totally useless, unnecessary death that has been a huge pain in many people.

Zygmunt Bauman defines this growing human suffering relegated to the status of "collaterals" as the most disastrous among countless potential problems that humanity may have to confront, contain and resolve during the current century "

Words from Marta Davi:

Osama was, and is, the desert. I met him while visiting this majestic, untamable, wild, elemental and unfathomable place. I went alone and there he was, together with my guide and driver, and his mere presence inspired a feeling of safety. He knew the desert, every corner of it, he was generous to its few inhabitants, enjoyed the nights, the stars and the silence. He was very capable, equipped to survive any adversity, and loved the desert. I shall never forget the love he felt for it and the desert loved him back.

It rained on us, it rained on us! For many, many years it had not rained and I shall never forget the sight of rain falling in the desert. It moved us all!

Thank you, Osama, for allowing me to share with you and get to know such a magical place and, above all, thank you for showing me how to truly appreciate and endlessly enjoy the silence, the peace and the serene beauty of this corner of beautiful and suffering Libya.

Osama/desert your memory will live on!

THE MAN OF THE DEEP GAZE

I remember long time ago, now it is like a distant dream, which I sometimes wonder what is real or imaginative, i met the man of the deep gaze.

The man of the deep gaze was sitting on a dune, along with a few friends and my aunt Leonor Massanet Arbona. He was wearing a djellaba, and his head was covered by a blue scarf that was screwed in the head. You could only see his eyes. At that instant, his black eyes shut directly into my soul.

I had heard for a long time talk about him, but I never had the pleasure to be in front of him before. It was like coming face to face with some character in a story. There he was, looking at me, and hoping that I make him any question.

At the beginning I didn't know what else to say, i hesitation, I was a bit shy because of the language and those penetrating eyes. He placed the djellaba, and show me a friendly smile. Suddenly the intimidating face became sweet, curiously familiar. His face showed tenderness and kindness. So plug in my tape recorder and we begin to talk about the situation in his country.

I saw a young man, but with a great weight on his backs, a man who felt responsible, not only of his family, but of its people. For a few moments I felt pity for him, I would liked that for a few moments he could removed the slab of the responsibility and I will give me as a present another friendly smile.

We went on talking, until one it came a time that he decided that we had to stop, and frankly it would not be me who was going to discuss that. The man of the gaze deep was very respectful. But this is the way that it should be, as he had to hold many things and people.

The days that continued I saw other aspects of him. We couldn't see much, since each one ran through the desert by their side, but sometimes he make the effort to come to our group. We watched the sun set in the dunes in silence, we played with the jeeps to reach the top of the highest dunes in the world, we danced beside the fire in the darkest night and with more stars that i have been able to get to see. Thus we could learn a little bit ... And I always will remember what he said to my aunt Leo, when she told me she was looking for a husband for me, only half-jokingly, half seriously: " Marta is free, leave it free". Words that surprise me a lot knowing his sisters.

Yes, his sisters, especially Ruba, a very important person for me , although we only met for a few hours, but dig deeply inside me, many days I am thinking about her, even now after so many yearst. When I met her i felt reflected on her. We were two reflections, two girls of the same age, university with very different lifes. We both connected much at that moment and felt very near.

Well, then I went, and the man of the penetrating eyes returned to become a character in the story which you listen stories. Sometimes he was visiting our island, other telling me that he had done. Then married, had children, and then…

... Then the war struck his life, and although to a much lesser level, ours too. For my part the war passed on me, something I had a hard time digesting or assuming. My aunt on the other hand faced it as a courageous, or as a fighter as it always has been. Even in times of war, the man of the penetrating gaze traveled to meet with her. I have just the war at a superficial level, the man of the penetrating gaze continued living with his family. And so the myth of the man of the gaze deep continued, as this story that you must count each night before going to sleep.

But I guess that not everything is forever, day January 22/ 2014, the man of the gaze deep, Osama, was kidnapped and found dead yesterday with a beaten and shot in the head.

Today I say goodbye you Osama, i do so publicly, for people to see what stupid that is a war, so stupid it is to do harm to people. Goodbye Osama, father, brother, friend, and the wise man of the gaze deep. Especially in honor of a heroine of the twenty-first century, my aunt Leonor Massanet

Marta Mezquida

Osama Abu-Bakr killed in Libya: condolences and requiem

Posted on Sunday, February 2, 2014 11:36

From Unity Journal we express our condolences to our companion Leonor Massanet in Libya for the murder of Osama Abu-Bakr, who was his friend and partner in the defense of that country and in denouncing those who revile.

Several days ago a Report noted saying he disappeared. We regret deeply that has come to confirm the worst fears about who opened the doors of Libya to Leonor. Today more than ever if possible, they should continue their invaluable task of showing the Libyan truth through the article, ethnography, psycho-social study, photography and filming. The truth is at this time of wolf devouring the country, backlit truth it was in recent times sovereignty, independence, collective enjoyment of wealth and prosperity.

Osama has been killed by the worms; essentially the same swarming around Miami, for certain neighborhoods of Caracas, hand-Henri Lévy in expensive hotels in Paris, or by state corridors of South Sudan. Le gunmen have killed a hegemony that almost ended with Libya, shocked as I was by the extraordinary human development in Libya to the mirror once and future African engine.

In its recent conference photo-exhibition in Barcelona, Leonor, invited by the Anti-imperialist Comitè, he told us and showed us the dignity and existential joy of a people belonging to himself. We showed and talked about the multitudinous tribal and inter-tribal councils; of the infrastructure; water; of factories and workshops; fields and wheat; of popular democracy; that pan-African currency that Gaddafi planned for transactions and trade the Black Continent replacing $ against Dictatorship of the WTO. A Libyan Jamahiriya reached hundreds of thousands people looking for that nonexistent future in their home countries. All were welcome, but not only with words. All participating Libya. Libya had life for all. All were benefited by the gratuity of the essential structures the day (energy and domestic resources) and decreed aid and maximum prices. Now Libya by sea, who can flee, thousands, drowning against Italian coast.

How would tolerate that African hegemony yankie example, all investments, all those social spending, when he is unable to invest in foreign capitals over-accumulated ?: destruction of Libya was neither more nor less than paradigm scorched earth policy. Aniquilatoria atrocious policy practiced to begin with the Libyan population (as human beings and their labor is the main productive force). So while the killing of Osama is one among hundreds of thousands already, yours is not "just another case" but all of them. The killing of Osama is the murder of a country, while political-military and propaganda operation killer could only culminate in the pulverized rubble on which the imperialists continue with how much killing is accurate to the enthronement of his worms.

We suffer here "our" worms supposedly "neo-leftist". That he calls "Casta", "sect", "terrorism", "Dictatorship", "oppression" ..., who naturally try to defend imperialist operations, both his people and the physical Nation whose frame of materiality and wealth the country must interact to produce their own social life. While, from their press and pages, called "Rebellion" and even "Libyan or Syrian revolution" Fascism applied by reactionary, brutal and sectarian fanatics, or simply as mercenaries and cynical playwrights as "our" worms. Why not ask the worms Libyan or Syrian which is the only real dictatorship in this matter ?; the Dictatorship of which they eat, drink, dress and walk through the sets and tables of "talking shop".

So from Unit Journal least I'll never vote for Pablito ask Iglesias and his (vivales, ricoachones, etc). Because if all this supposed "neo-left" venal not been dedicated to lie ("Gaddafi Dictator", "Assad Tyrant", "Mursi is like Allende", blah blah blah ...), then perhaps the popular sectors of "public opinion" would not have been so stunned by the imperialist barbarism in progress.And who knows maybe !: People, as it moved against the attack on Iraq, would have moved in the streets against these "revolutions" of Zionism and the CIA. I know that probably this alternative scenario, in the streets of Madrid, Barcelona, London, Paris or Washington, did not influence on a US State Department decided to throw miles, as in Iraq. But the massive electoral pressure and therefore perhaps it could have inhibited a Spanish Governments like to keep as

211

submissive fold the Zionist plan of domestication, blood and fire, and dissidents United Arab nations.

I also know that, after all, are very decisive and rather marginal these little characters "left" languages tiller against any State, political and institutional system that imperialism has in Blacklist. But they are, after all, disseminators, among the ranks of the People of the imperialist doctrine of the Axis of Evil. Therefore, a single vote. Because meanness is the need to give your side and fight for itself; no matter how deep or superficial in its effects and consequences. Because we owe it to the memory of Osama Abu-Bakr, Libyan, Syrian, Sudanese, Egyptians, Palestinians, Tunisians ... victims of their social-imperialist "spokespersons". Because, to paraphrase García Lorca, behind each figure subsidized the slanderers of Peoples and Governments dissidents "there is a drop of blood duck".

Tamer Sarkis Fernández,
Vice-Director of DAILY UNIT

Words from Otta Jiri

I met Osama on few occasions only.

First it was in on our trip to Libya in 2007.

He was a head of a "desert group" who took us to deep south

of Libya.

I was lucky to sit for about a week in the back of a car driven by Osama through Akakos mountains and Awbari sands.

This first time I just admired his incredible talent to find the way through the Sahara.

We didn´t speak much. My Arabic was (and still is) very poor (just few words) and I didn´t know he spoke English.

Nevertheless we felt his authority over the other members of his team and we felt very safe (even though we knew desert was a dangerous environment).

I remember one moment when he drove his Toyota (with us inside) over the edge of a dune a bit faster than needed and we jumped hitting the nose of the car into the sand on the other side.

We were really scared. But he gently comforted my wife and was so calm that after few minutes we just laughed over the incident.

That was the time I realized he was a real gentleman.

My second time was in 2010 (you surely remember the difficult time with entry visa), I had to cancel my group visit (the friends couldn´t postpone the time any more).

And because I really wanted to do the visit – I took my 82 years old mother, my wife and her mother and we did a "family trip".

That time Osama organized his friends to take care of us (he was engaged with other group deep in Sahara).

But he took his time, drove from Sabha to Ghadames just to meet us for a few minutes.

My wife cannot forget their first meeting in the lobby of a Ghadames hotel.

She entered the lobby and she was met by a dark handsome gentleman dressed in the traditional Saharan (Touareg ?) dress, spotless brown, ironed (even though he has just arrived from the distance over 700 km through Sahara). She was really impressed by his cultivated appearance and friendly approach. And we both were surprised that after those few minutes of personal talk he jumped into the car and drove back somewhere to Sabha.

The third time – it was in February 2011 - was the most dramatic.

My group (two men and four women) arrived to Tripoli on February 18th, few days after the riots begun in Benghazi.

After two busy days in Tripoli we started – still in care of one of Osama´s friends (unfortunately I don´t remember the name) for Ghadames.

Some 50 km before Ghadames we turned back as the phone report to the driver said it wouldn´t be safe to drive further.

After more phone calls from Osama we spent the night in a house of another friend of friend (whose family was taken somewhere else just to make comfort to us).

The next day we drove to Sabha. Early evening the car stopped on the road, we transferred to two Toyotas (driven by Osama and Mohammed) and both cars started directly into Sahara.

Night, sandy dunes in the car headlights, few shrubs. After (how many ?) kilometres we set the tents, Osama prepared the dinner for us and Mohammed boiled his famous tea.

It was calm, stars above – Sahara.

The next week we spent in the Awbari desert.

Osama driving, explaining, talking about Saharan culture, ways of life, how to keep alive, how to find water.

I doubted his words – I said "No. Impossible. You cannot find water here."

At that moment Osama stopped the car and said "If you dig here for about one meter deep you will find water." He took a small bowl and started digging.

We all took turns and indeed ! In the depth of arm´s reach we found water !

Absolutely incredible to us.

After a week we had to go to the civilization to tank the cars.

We were not allowed to go further and had to cancel the rest of our trip.

The drive to Sabha airport was a bit sad, but the situation in Libya was tense and not right for tourism.

Sabha airport was under the siege of thousands of foreign workers trying to find the way home.

We tried to get support from our embassy but the people there were busy to save themselves. They couldn't help us.

But even though the situation looked dangerous we didn't have that feeling. Osama was very calm and his composure radiated

 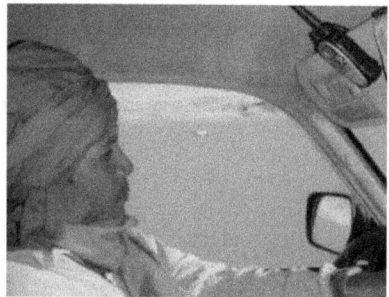

safety.

He did many calls, meetings and moves to get us safely home.

We spent two days in front of Sabha airport (you can imagine those thousands of men there and our four women sharing the social facilities ...).

And Osama did all to make our stay comfortable. And

finally he succeeded !!!

He got us on board of the only civilian aircraft flying from Sabha out of Libya in last seven days. To Cairo, Egypt.

In that situation that was a real heroic deed !

We cried when we were leaving.

We wished good future to him and his family ...

I was hoping to go and meet Osama again.

We agreed he will take us to Akakos – the part we had to cancel in 2011.

Even though we met just few times in our lives, we miss Osama very much.

He was the best guide I ever met. And not just guide – a cultured, sensitive, empathic, educated, reliable, brave man.

We will miss him.

Dear Leonor, if you find a way how to do something for his family, let me know.

Be brave

Jiri

....

I still admire Osama and his calmness through the tense situation in the early days of the unrest in February 2011.

He and Mohammed followed the news on the radio (extending its the antenna by some length of naked wire and a metal tray).

The most tense time for us were the days and night in front of empty Sabha airport with those thousands of foreign workers around us.

Osama organized his friends to guard us and be of any assistance that could have be needed.

In between he run through all his resources to get us out of the situation.

He even discussed with the director of the airport, with the head of security there, with the representatives of the companies who had their people there.

I can hardly imagine the effort and stress he must have felt.

My friend Frank (the other man in my group) didn´t make it any easier for Osama. Frank always pushed Osama to do more and more.

I tried to convince Frank that Osama is not a man to be pushed; he was doing his best.

Osama himself told me in one intimate moment that my words "We are in your hands, my friend" were the highest imperative for him.

I don´t know how he did it but he managed to get us into the one and only flight that left Sabha in the last week. unbelivable.

Osama was really the most reliable man I ever met.

As I wrote before: I met Osama just few times, I spent two individual weeks with him.

But I felt very close to him.

I think my feelings were caused mainly by his unforced authority, calmness, friendliness, knowledge and human understanding.

I will miss him !!!

Jiri

Words from Manuel

Osama I met him in person when I traveled to Libya in 2008.

I had already heard a lot about him, I had been told that he was a desert man, committed to his family, their traditions, their culture, their beliefs.

I lived with him a week in which he guided me through the

desert and made me really fascinating places.

On that trip I could feel how serious he was,and a person who was easy to trust. He did not talk much, but I could feel his inner peace from the beginning.

Every morning get up early to do their prayers, always discreet, and seemed very connected with nature, which always showed a deep respect.

Despite being young, showed mature, it is unfolded with skill in different situations were finding from finding alternatives to the inability to fly like we planned, or think of ways to meet our requests, to get us out of places that seemed inaccessible unaltered or lose patience.

My Week with Osama was rewarding for many reasons, I finish that week with the certainty that this world would be much better if there were more people like him

Manuel Contreras

Words from Eva

Anybody could feel that Osama was a man of the desert. The desert was his home, he moved into it with the confidence that comes from knowledge of the environment, but also with respect to who knows the silent dangers to humans in such immensity.

Osama knew how to find the path where the untrained western urbanites eye were neither able to capture the skyline.

Osama knew where the lush enough to shelter from the harsh African sun tree was noon. Osama knew that sector within the desert dunes could pitch your tent to rest in the night.

Osama knew how to prepare the Sahara green tea with lots of sugar under the cloak starry night sky, he knew how to pour in the tiny vessels from the pot without a drop is lost and while Osama slowly sipped with his soft voice was telling us his version of the legends of the Koran.

The beauty of metaphors contained in the book which we do not understand anything because our Western education has taught us to see the world differently. I remember that he told us about how to free the poison if you were bitten by a scorpion and prayers were said while waiting to be spit wound viscosity malignant poison before it reached the blood.

That beautiful stories! For me as a personal version of the Arabian Nights lived in my own flesh and blood, it was like a gift that was not expected.

Friend Osama your memory in my heart will always be attached to the desert. When we said goodbye at the airport I promised to return, and still hope to return when the madness destructive has to stop cruelty to humans countries desert.

I hope to keep my promise and relive the magic of the desert but sadly I I will not be able hear your voice because you have gone too early. But I will know your elegant and haughty figure dressed in screaming and turban will be in the shadow of the dunes under the reflection of the stars.

Goodbye my friend Osama

Eva Bastida Tobau

IN MEMORY OF OSAMA

I tried many times to write my feelings and thought I keep from Osama but it is very difficult to describe who he was, because

when you meet Osama you can not express with the words what he has left in our hearts.

It all started in September 2007 during a trip to Libya, fate led us to choose between two conductors, we chose him. Immediately there was a mutual understanding despite our difficulties due to language differences.

At the end of our journey together with a gesture or a look and a thousand laughs we understood very well each other even without talking. We left Libya with a hug and a promise to meet again in Italy, in my house.

So it was in April 2008, Osama was my guest for a few

days, were unforgettable days, including spaghetti, stories, and experiences in the wilderness.

Thus was born the idea of a second and longer trip to Libya in October 2008. This second visit was the real journey in the desert where we could appreciate the beautiful scenery but especially our relationship with Osama as a man born and raised in the desert.

I was struck by their confidence in dealing with any situation and its proverbial "no problem" was a guarantee of peace for us all. Met a lot of confidence and esteem every day and our friendship became increasingly deep enough to consider ourselves brothers. The most striking feature of Osama was the love of the wilderness, for his land for his Libya and all its inhabitants, dreamed big things to get better and better, helping others before himself, and here's your second and greatest feature it was unique: the great love for his family, his only purpose in life. Ready to help anyone in trouble, brothers sisters dreamed so many children around, a large family the same as where he was born.

For us who are accustomed to live more selfishly based on different concepts, it was difficult for us to understand some of their positions. Willing to die to defend their "tribe" of their land, their increasingly threatened by the "conquistadores" modern thirst for wealth devastate ready to steal and kill the rightful owners country. And so it was .... !!!

Osama is dead without betraying his large, deep ideals of peace and respect for humility, family and love of neighbor.

We talked on the phone every two weeks to greet us and strengthen our friendship dreaming that we would meet again to have tea together on the dunes, an appointment that will never come .... !!!!.

I could write hours about him and all we live together, but I think that's enough, I hope that someday their young children Zaid and Abubaker can read this and be proud of a father who has not had time to embrace them and raise them in his image and deserve.

Rest in peace my only brother. Goodbye

Franco

Words from "the three women"

Osama, its so dificult to tell you goodbye. So we tell you "see

you soon".

You welcome us in your country, you welcomed us and together with you, we discover and share the beauty of the desert. We can not forget the starry nights, meals that you and your Coky were praparing, Akako stones, paint, light, the color of the earth and especially your smile and your love for Libya.

Looking at the photos we remembered the trip we share and we only have words of thanks

.

 With this song we tell you: " see you forever and ever"

Ways that now fade

Ways that we have to follow alone,

226

Ways next to the stars,

Ways that are not now.

We leave all, the burning heard through the world,

Over the Love walls, over the skin

We were two fire birds, seeding storms,

Now we are two son of the sun, on the desert

Never its too late to start again,
To seek out treasure
Ways, dreams and promises .

Ways that are new
Its not easy to know where you have to go,
Take the direcction of your heart.

Never its too late to start again,
To seek out treasure.

Ways that now fade,

Ways that we have to follow alone,

Ways next to the satars,

Ways that are not now.

"Camins" de Sopa de cabra.

Marisa,Pilar,Pilar